THE
BIRDS

A Full-Length Play by
Aristophanes
arranged for the stage
by WALTER KERR

THE DRAMATIC PUBLISHING COMPANY

THE BIRDS

A Full-length Play for
a Flexible Cast

CHARACTERS

PITHETAERUS THE FOOTLOOSE, a crappel
EUELPIDES THE FOOTSORE, a fearling
TROCHILUS, the Butler Bird
EPOPS, King of the Birds
PROCNE THE NIGHTINGALE, wife to Epops
LEADER OF THE CHORUS
PRIEST-BIRD
POET
PROPHET
REAL ESTATE MAN
INSPECTOR
LAWYER
FIRST MESSENGER
SECOND MESSENGER
IRIS THE SWIFT, a small-time Goddess
HERALD
PROMPTER, offstage voice
PROMETHEUS
HERCULES
BARBARIAN GOD
NEPTUNE
CHORUS of BIRDS

TIME: About 414 B.C.

PLACE: A rugged mountain-top, some distance from Athens.

EDITOR'S NOTE

Aristophanes, writing in Athens in the fifth century B.C., is acknowledged to be the father of all western comedy, and, perhaps along with Moliere, to be one of its two greatest masters. Yet his plays are almost never produced.

It is popularly assumed that the extreme license and bawdry permitted to Athenian comic writers is the principal reason why the plays are not often seen in our time. Strictly speaking, this is not true. Vulgarity has always been a part of the comic vein, and even its Athenian extremes can usually be restated in a manner not too offensive to modern ears. The real difficulty encountered in staging Aristophanic comedy lies in the abundance of explicit contemporary reference - content which we should need a history-book to follow, and without which we often miss the joke. By the time this "obscure" material has been cut from an Aristophanic play, often too little remains for a full evening in the theatre.

The Birds is fortunate in this respect. Aside from being one of the least bawdy and most lyrical of the plays, it is also, in its original form, one of the longest and most developed. When the play has been cut, a substantial body of comic incident remains.

Another difficulty encountered in producing Aristophanes is that of translation. Though we now have some translations of Greek tragedy which may be considered adequate, comedy continues to suffer the numbing effects of stilted, pedantic, or merely literal renderings. An "acting edition" is necessary.

The present acting edition is neither a new translation from the Greek nor an attempt to sustain the entire play in verse. Both these eventualities are desirable, but they constitute a project of much greater scope than that attempted here, and in any case the problem of doing justice to Aristophanes the poet will only be solved, when it is solved, by a poet of like calibre.

The present editor has simply tried to make a practicable stage version of *The Birds* with the materials now at hand, in the hope that actual production will stimulate the kind of interest needed to bring forth further - and better - adaptations and translations. He has, therefore, compared a wide variety of older translations, reduced the lines of the play to their simplest meanings, and then recast these lines in a colloquial vein. The intention has been to make the play sound more or less as it might have sounded to an average Athenian sitting in a popular comic theatre, thoroughly familiar with the comic devices and the patois of his author.

The editor has further cut away those parts of the text which are now obscure and, to compensate for this cutting, has here and there extended an idea which may be found in the original in more cursory fashion. Sometimes these elaborations are fairly extensive, and a good many liberties have been taken in the effort to pull the cut script together; but none of these elaborations is without some foundation in the text. The joke is *in* Aristophanes; our problem is to get it out where we can hear it.

The choruses of the play have been cut and blended from two earlier translations: that of J. H. Frere (1840) and that of Benjamin Bickley Rogers (1902).

The Birds (414 B.C.) was Aristophanes' first Utopian play. He was to write many more, before he was through expressing his contempt for the society of his day and his dream of a better one. In this instance, he has his "comedy team" leave Athens, fed up with the frauds and bores of that society, in an effort to found a better society among the birds. To do so, they must first locate Epops, King of the Birds, who was once a man like themselves and who might be expected to know both sides of the problem. How they find him and what they persuade him to do is the body of the play, here divided into two acts to correspond with its division of subject matter. The first act concerns the founding of Cloud Cuckoo-land and its triumph over all earthly bores and quacks. The second concerns its triumph over the Olympian gods, and contains Aristophanes' comment on the polytheistic absurdities to which Athenian religion had been reduced.

This acting version was first presented at the Catholic University of America, Washington, D.C., in 1948.

W.K.

ACT ONE

SCENE: *PITHETAERUS and EUELPIDES appear DL, as though climbing from the earth below. PITHETAERUS carries a crow in his arms, EUELPIDES a jay. Both are exhausted from the long climb. Before they can relax, however, Euelpides' jay begins pecking its head vigorously toward C.*

EUELPIDES *(listening to his jay)*. Straight ahead, you say? To the tree over there? *(The jay nods excitedly and EUELPIDES starts C. As PITHETAERUS follows him, his own crow begins wagging its head violently in another direction.)*

PITHETAERUS. Oh, this damn pigeon! *(To the bird.)* What do you say now? Go two miles *back? (PITHETAERUS howls with disgust and collapses on a rock, near L. EUELPIDES comes to him, shaking his finger at the crow.)*

EUELPIDES. Listen, bird. You're supposed to be guiding us. But all we do is go backwards and sideways. We haven't got that kind of time. *(The crow bites his shaking finger and he leaps away, nursing it.)*

PITHETAERUS. To think that I - a mature man! - should travel a hundred miles with a bird giving me directions! *(His crow sets up a violent jerking and EUELPIDES comes in warily to listen.)*

EUELPIDES *(interpreting)*. He says it isn't far as the crow flies. *(PITHETAERUS looks at the crow in disgust, begins slapping its head vigorously; the crow bites him. EUELPIDES, surveying the rocky terrain)*. Personally, I'm worn down to my toenails.

PITHETAERUS. If I only knew where we were--

EUELPIDES *(wistfully)*. Suppose we could ever find our way home again?

PITHETAERUS. No.

EUELPIDES. Oh, dear.

PITHETAERUS *(sudden renewal of determination).* And if I could I wouldn't want to!

EUELPIDES. Oh, dear.

PITHETAERUS *(on his feet again, looking around).* I wonder what road this is.

EUELPIDES. Oh, dear. *(Helpfully.)* It's the Oh Dear Road. *(PITHETAERUS swats him one, he dodges; he then takes it out on his jay, swatting the bird as he continues.)* A lot of good you are! *(Calling to PITHETAERUS, who is wandering about the stage.)* I told you we couldn't trust that bird-seller. Telling us these fellows would just naturally lead us to the King of the Birds! *(Sits down, C, despondently.)* I don't think they ever heard of the King of the Birds. And if they did, I'll bet they're disloyal. *(Jay opens his mouth.)* Don't open your face like that! You look anything but attractive. *(Jay's head begins jutting toward R.)* Where? Where? Over there? *(His eyes glued to the jay, he quickly rises and moves in the indicated direction.)* All right. All right. I'm going. Keep showing me. *(He walks smack into a wall of rock, rebounds, turns on the jay.)* That's rock! Oh, you knew that! That's what you had in mind! *(Begins to throttle his jay. PITHETAERUS, who has been wandering UC, peering off at the highest point of the rocks with his back to us, now seems to be engaged in some excitement with his bird.)* Find something? What's your bird doing?

PITHETAERUS *(in a rage).* Biting my damn fingers off!

EUELPIDES. Any road up there?

PITHETAERUS. Nothing. No road anywhere.

EUELPIDES. Oh, dear. I haven't got a nerve left. I've used up every single nerve trying to go to the birds, and now they're all gone. *(He shudders violently.)* See? *(Turns to the audience, comes down toward them.)* I suppose you wonder what we're doing here? I wonder, too. *(Keeping up a direct conversation with the audience, he now goes to L where they have entered, and hauls over a couple of heavy sacks filled with equipment. He drags these across stage, with great effort, and deposits them at extreme DR, meanwhile continuing the conversation.)* You probably think we're crazy. We are. We come of very good families. Legitimate. We were very respected people back home. Athens. Very fine city. You probably think we were thrown out. *(Shakes his head.)* Just got up and left. Walked out. Still walking. We don't hate Athens. Fine city. Rich, too. Everybody equal. Every man has absolute freedom to pay taxes. Every man has a constitutional right to ruin himself. *(These are read as though they were virtues; now his face falls.)* Of course, the town's full of lawyers. Always suing everybody. Government men, too. And inspectors. Always inspectors! *(PITHETAERUS has momentarily abandoned his search above to listen to these last remarks; now he adds his own complaints, coming down to EUELPIDES and sitting down while EUELPIDES continues doing all the work.)*

PITHETAERUS. Tell 'em about the real estate. Tell 'em about the long-haired poets!

EUELPIDES. He's right. The city's infested. A lot of prophets, too. Always predicting what's going to happen the day after tomorrow. Very wearing.

PITHETAERUS. Bores, bores, bores!

EUELPIDES. That's why we left.

PITHETAERUS. Get away from the bores, get a little peace!

EUELPIDES. That's why we're looking for the King of the Birds. *(His work finished, coming down to the audience again.)* If *anybody* should know of a nice quiet place where a couple of men could settle - with no bores - it should be the King of the Birds. Birds get around. *(PITHETAERUS suddenly jumps up, attending to his crow.)*

PITHETAERUS. My bird's doing something!

EUELPIDES. I'll bet I know what.

PITHETAERUS *(excited, moving anxiously wherever the bird indicates, but never more than a few steps in any one direction)*. No... no, watch!

EUELPIDES *(indifferently and sadly, to the audience, playing against Pithetaerus' excitement)*. So we started off with a stewpot, a knife and fork - a few myrtle berries - and, now you know.

PITHETAERUS. Here! Look!

EUELPIDES *(to his jay, laconically)*. Has that other bird really got anything? *(The jay shakes its head slowly, with contempt.)*

PITHETAERUS. It's behaving like there were other birds around somewhere! *(Now Euelpides' bird becomes agitated.)*

EUELPIDES. Mine's doing it, too! Where? Where? *(He runs agitatedly wherever his bird indicates, so that both PITHETAERUS and EUELPIDES are scurrying hither and thither independently. Suddenly they cross each other unexpectedly, so that EUELPIDES gives a little scream of fright, then calms down as he sees it is PITHETAERUS.)* Oh, it's you.

PITHETAERUS. Yes, dammit, it's me! Look for some birds!

EUELPIDES. Maybe we could scare them up if we made some noise.

PITHETAERUS *(indicating rock RC)*. That's right. Here... kick your leg against that rock.

EUELPIDES *(responds automatically, about to do it, then considers)*. Wouldn't it be louder if we used your head?

PITHETAERUS *(roaring)*. Kick your leg against that rock!

EUELPIDES *(resignedly)*. All right. *(Braces himself and does it; lets out a great series of yowls.)*

PITHETAERUS *(listening to the yowls with approval)*. That's fine. That ought to do it. *(Motioning EUELPIDES to join him.)* Ready, now. They'll be coming.

(Together they move warily, expectantly, among the rocks UR. Coming on from UL, we see TROCHILUS, the Butler Bird, entering matter-of-factly, nose in air. He turns around a rock unexpectedly and comes face to face with PITHETAERUS and EUELPIDES. ALL leap into the air in terror of each other, screaming and chattering, and dive for hiding places. PITHETAERUS and EUELPIDES hide in the rock formation at R, TROCHILUS high on the rock formation at L.)

EUELPIDES. Mercy have Apollo. I mean, Apollo have mercy. *(His teeth chatter.)*

PITHETAERUS *(peeping over a ledge, trembling)*. What a beak!

TROCHILUS *(waveringly, from his hiding place)*. Men! Bird-catchers!

PITHETAERUS *(trying to get up nerve, his voice faltering)*. H-ho there! D-d-don't be frightened of us!

TROCHILUS *(adopting the same bravura, calling across)*. F-f-frightened of you? F-f-frightened of men? *(Bats his wings at them.)* Y-y-you're done for!

EUELPIDES *(helpfully)*. Oh... we're not men! *(To himself.)* No. Never say that.

TROCHILUS *(relaxing)*. You're not? What are you, then?

EUELPIDES *(indicating PITHETAERUS)*. Well, I don't know about him, but I'm a bird. An African bird. The... the Fearling.

TROCHILUS. Never heard of him. *(Becoming braver, taking command.)* And what kind of a bird is that bird? Huh?

PITHETAERUS *(half-rising from behind ledge)*. Why, I'm a... *(Pauses to consider, then with some self-disgust.)* ...a Crapple, if you must know.

EUELPIDES. One of the yellow-bellied school.

PITHETAERUS *(regaining confidence)*. Now, see here. You're a bit of a fright yourself. What are you?

TROCHILUS *(coming down the rock, manservant style)*. I am a butler bird. Butler to Epops, King of the Birds.

EUELPIDES *(excited)*. He's our man! *(Trochilus' head whips around, alert.)* I mean, bird.

TROCHILUS. Choose your language.

PITHETAERUS *(tentatively coming down from the rock formation)*. Would you... do us the kindness to call your master?

TROCHILUS. I'm sorry. He has just fallen asleep after a dainty supper of berries, and a few choice grubs. I picked the grubs myself.

EUELPIDES *(relaxed now, assuming an air)*. Wake him up. Tell him we're here.

TROCHILUS. He will be angry.

PITHETAERUS (taking a deep breath). We'll risk it.

TROCHILUS. Very well. *(Starts to go; L above, pauses to check.)* The Fearling, and the...

PITHETAERUS *(obligingly)*. Crapple.

TROCHILUS. Crapple. I think I understand. *(TROCHILUS goes, UL. PITHETAERUS and EUELPIDES follow him a step or two, completely off the rock formation; then PITHETAERUS turns on EUELPIDES and kicks him to DR.)*

PITHETAERUS. You mouse! You flyspeck! What were you so frightened about? You were so frightened you made me frightened. What was the matter with you?

EUELPIDES. I was frightened.

PITHETAERUS. Where's your jay? You were so frightened, you big coward, you let your jay go!

EUELPIDES. Where's your crow?

PITHETAERUS *(realizing he no longer has his crow)*. I gave him his freedom.

EUELPIDES. That was decent of you.

(There is a sudden loud whirr and EPOPS rises to the top of a rock at the highest stage point, UC. PITHETAERUS and EUELPIDES realize that something has happened. Slowly they turn to face EPOPS, above. When they have finally turned full face to him, they collapse in a trembling heap together, and scurry on hands and knees for the shelter of a DR rock.)

EPOPS *(in a great voice)*. Who wants me?

EUELPIDES *(terrified, trying to laugh it off)*. I can't imagine. *(To PITHETAERUS.)* Did you see anybody?

EPOPS. Does someone dare to laugh at the King of the Birds?

EUELPIDES. No... no... just a little giddy... *(Shoving PITHE-TAERUS, as though to start him running out of this place.)* Giddyap. *(PITHETAERUS collapses into Euelpides' arms; EUELPIDES is struggling to hold him up during the ensuing conversation.)*

EPOPS. You must know, strangers, that I once was a man.

EUELPIDES *(looking down at PITHETAERUS)*. We all were.

EPOPS. Born of woman, married to a wife, I was unfaithful to my dear Procne. Now I am changed by Apollo into a bird, and Procne is the nightingale, and I am faithful at last.

EUELPIDES *(to the audience)*. We're certainly getting the exposition out.

EPOPS. Who are you?

EUELPIDES. Mortals. Haven't had any affairs with nightingales.

EPOPS. From what country?

EUELPIDES. The land of democracy, where everyone is equal.

EPOPS *(suddenly suspicious)*. You're not government men?

EUELPIDES. Anti-government men.

EPOPS *(relaxing, moving gracefully across bridge at L so that he can see them better from across the stage)*. They're getting around to that, are they?

EUELPIDES. Not fast enough. That's why we came.

EPOPS. Why have you come? *(PITHETAERUS, in Euelpides' arms, begins to stir.)*

PITHETAERUS. What? What?

EUELPIDES. He wants to know why we came.

PITHETAERUS. Tell him.

EUELPIDES. If you can lie down somewhere else, I will. *(Drops PITHETAERUS with a thud and goes to C, speaking up to EPOPS on the bridge at mid-L. PITHETAERUS crawls to a small rock and sits down.)* We came to see you.

EPOPS. Why me?

EUELPIDES *(taking on graces and airs, in the manner of a rather florid ambassador)*. Because formerly you were a man, as we are. Formerly you had debts, as we do. And formerly you did not want to pay them, as we don't. Furthermore, now that you're a bird, you must have flown everywhere. And while you were flying all over the world, you must have seen - somewhere - some little town, where a man can sit back, stretch out, drop a berry into his mouth... *(Pantomimes what he describes.)*

PITHETAERUS *(chiming in)*. ...and not be bothered with bores!

EPOPS. Are you looking for a city greater than your own?

EUELPIDES. No, not a greater one. Just one more pleasant to live in.

PITHETAERUS *(nodding)*. No bores.

EPOPS. What sort of city would please you?

EUELPIDES. I'll tell you. A city where the following would be the most important business transacted: Some friend would come banging on your door at a reasonable hour in the morning, and say: *(Dramatizing, in a harsh voice.)* "Get up! Get your wife and children! Get over to my house. Sit down at my table and eat till you bust. And if you don't, I'll be mad at you!" I have something like that in mind.

EPOPS. I see. Sort of... roughing it?

EUELPIDES. Yes.

EPOPS *(to PITHETAERUS)*. And you?

PITHETAERUS. My tastes are similar.

EPOPS. I see. As a matter of fact, there is a city like that. It's on the Red Sea.

PITHETAERUS *(rising, asserting himself now)*. No, no! No sea ports. Let a ship dock, and there'll be a process server on it. Someplace remote. Uninhabited. Inaccessible. *(Has been envisioning such a place as he speaks; suddenly there is a gleam in his eye.)* Wait a minute. Now, wait a minute!

EUELPIDES *(resignedly)*. You have an idea.

PITHETAERUS. Yes!

EUELPIDES. The last idea you had was using birds for guides. I hate to bring it up.

PITHETAERUS *(excited)*. No, listen, now. Listen! *(Grabs EUELPIDES by the shoulders and sits him down between himself and EPOPS, who moves slightly down on his rock perch.)*

EUELPIDES. It isn't as though I had a choice. *(To the audience.)* You do. You can go home anytime.

PITHETAERUS *(striding around, his eyes ablaze as he works out his plan)*. Sh-h-h-h!

EUELPIDES *(relaying it unnecessarily to the audience)*. Sh-h-h-h!

PITHETAERUS *(ready to talk now, becoming momentously confidential with EPOPS)*. Tell me. What is it like to live with the birds themselves?

EPOPS. What?

PITHETAERUS. You ought to know. What's the life like?

EPOPS *(rising and moving on the bridge as he considers)*. Why, it's not a bad sort of life. Of course, you have no money.

EUELPIDES. I'm as good as a bird now. *(PITHETAERUS kicks him.)*

EPOPS. And, naturally, you have none of the problems that go with money.

EUELPIDES. That's logical. *(PITHETAERUS kicks him.)*

EPOPS. The food is nice. White sesame, myrtle, poppies, mint--

EUELPIDES. Worms. *(PITHETAERUS about to kick him, EUELPIDES quickly walks, without making himself erect, from one rock to another.)*

PITHETAERUS *(grandiosely)*. I am beginning to conceive a great plan. *(To EPOPS, moving up the rocks at R toward him.)* All you have to do is take my advice.

EPOPS. Take your advice? How?

PITHETAERUS *(after a significant pause)*. Found a city!

EPOPS. A city for birds? What kind of city could we have?

PITHETAERUS *(dragging EPOPS to high point UC)*. Oh, come on, come on! Don't be a fool. Here. Look down. *(EPOPS bends over the high point and looks down, then waits for PITHETAERUS to say something more; he doesn't.)*

EPOPS. I'm looking.

PITHETAERUS. Now look up.

EPOPS *(repeats business)*. I'm looking.

PITHETAERUS. Turn your head around. *(EPOPS does, twisting his head.)* Well! What do you find?

EPOPS. That my neck is getting stiff.

PITHETAERUS. No, no! What do you *see?*

EPOPS. The same old clouds and sky.

PITHETAERUS *(as though it were quite simple)*. That's it! The land of the birds!

EPOPS. I knew that.

EUELPIDES *(still below, indifferent)*. *I* knew that. He gets excited about nothing.

PITHETAERUS. But you can turn it into a city!

EPOPS *(incredulous)*. A city in the air?

PITHETAERUS. Surround it with walls and fortify it!

EUELPIDES *(to audience)*. He's going to surround space.

EPOPS. What for?

PITHETAERUS. To seize all the power of the universe... for yourself. For the birds. *(Offhand.)* And, of course, we'll have a little share in it, too. *(The salesman again.)* You can reign over mankind as you now do over grasshoppers! You can rule the gods!

EPOPS. How?

PITHETAERUS. By starving them into submission.

EPOPS. I don't follow you.

EUELPIDES. You're not the first.

PITHETAERUS. Now, listen! When men are on their last legs, when they're desperate... what is the only thing that can help them?

EPOPS. The gods.

PITHETAERUS. And how do they get the gods to help them?

EPOPS *(indicating a small altar-like rock DL of C)*. By offering sacrifice. They put a goat or an ox in the sacrificial fire.

PITHETAERUS *(moving downstage with EPOPS and dramatizing what he says).* And the smoke rises up through the air until it reaches the heavens. The gods notice it, and come to the rescue. Is that right? *(EPOPS nods.)* Listen carefully. In the practical business affairs of Earth, suppose I am a man living in this country. *(Marks out an area on the ground with his foot; EUELPIDES jumps up and puts his foot in the area, helpfully.)* But I want to go to that country over there on business. *(Indicates an area some distance toward R.)* Between the two countries is a middle country which I must pass through. *(EUELPIDES starts to travel toward the second area through middle area, but PITHETAERUS stops him midway.)* Now, when I want to pass through it, what do I have to do?

EPOPS. Pay tribute.

PITHETAERUS. Precisely! *(EUELPIDES reaches for his purse, but it is empty; shrugs, goes away and sits down, L.)* Now here is all that smoke going through *your* country for nothing. But if you build a wall and fortify it, you can demand that men acknowledge you as rulers of the universe and pay you a tribute. Otherwise, *you don't let the smoke through! (He pauses for EPOPS and EUELPIDES to grasp and admire this notion.)* In addition, with no smoke coming up, the gods starve to death. You rule the universe!

EPOPS *(his imagination fired, darting about the stage).* By snares! By networks! By cages! That's the cleverest idea I've ever heard. I've been wanting to get back at that Apollo. *(Faces them.)* If I can get the approval of the other birds, I'll do it.

PITHETAERUS. Will you explain the matter to them?

EPOPS. No, *you* will. You're a splendid talker.

EUELPIDES. Splendid.

PITHETAERUS. How will you get them all together?

EPOPS. No trouble at all. I shall awaken dear Procne, my nightingale. Once they hear our voices, they will come to us hot on the wing!

PITHETAERUS. Then hurry, my dear fellow, hurry. Wake up Procne!

(Begin MUSIC. EPOPS waves them aside as he goes to the nest in the rocks. PITHETAERUS and EUELPIDES scurry DL of C and conceal themselves, watching. EPOPS makes several birdlike sounds and the nest door slowly opens, or unfolds. PROCNE is discovered asleep. Slowly she wakes. Moving from the nest, she dances drowsily, waking herself, as EPOPS speaks softly.)

EPOPS. Chase off drowsy sleep, my mate!
    Shake off thy slumbers, and clear and strong
    Let loose thy flood of glorious song.
    With the liquid note of thy tawny throat
    Through the leafy curls of the woodbine sweet
    Send thy pure sound to the heavenly seat
    Of Phoebus, lord of the golden lair,
    Who lists to thy wild plaint echoing there.
    Draw answering strains from Phoebus' lyre
    Till he stirs the dance of the aerial choir
    And calls from the blessed lips on high
    Of a thousand birds, divine reply
    To the tones of thy witching melody--

EUELPIDES *(as PROCNE now stands erect, ready to call)*. Oh, by Zeus, what a sweet little bird. I'm charmed, charmed.

PITHETAERUS. Sh-h!

EUELPIDES. What's the matter?

PITHETAERUS. The King is ready. Procne is ready. They're going to call the birds! *(During the ensuing passage PROCNE takes the lead, moving in dance rhythm to each promontory on the set and singing a birdlike strain. EPOPS, also in dance rhythms, moves to each position after her, keeping on a lower level.)*

PROCNE. Apopopoi popoi popopopoi popoi!

EPOPS. Come hither any bird with plumage like my own,
    Come hither ye that fatten on the acres newly sown,
    On the acres by the farmer newly sown.
    And the myriad tribes that feed on the barley and the seed
    The tribes that lightly fly, giving out a gentle cry--

PROCNE *(on another promontory)*.
    Tio, tio, tio, tio, tiotinx!

EPOPS. And ye who in the gardens pleasant harvest glean
 Lurking in the branches of the ivy ever green
 And ye who top the mountains with gay and airy flight,
 Come hither one and all, come flying to our call--
PROCNE. Trioto, trioto, totobrinx!
CHORUS *(off faintly).*
 Trioto, trioto, totobrinx!
 *(Faintly a whirring of wings begins off, and the stage begins to
 darken as though from a sky filled with approaching birds.)*
EPOPS. Ye that snap up the gnats, shrilly voiced,
 Mid the deep water-glens of the fens,
 And the bird with the gay mottled plumes, come away--
PROCNE. Francolin! Francolin!
EPOPS. Come away!
CHORUS *(off, louder).*
 Tio, tio, tio, tiotinx.
PITHETAERUS. See any birds yet?
EUELPIDES. No, but I've got my eyes open.
PITHETAERUS. That's your mouth, stupid. *(EPOPS and
 PROCNE now take up a kingly position together on the rock
 tower at R and remain still. EPOPS speaks climactically, as the
 music and the offstage whirring become louder.)*
EPOPS *(majestically).*
 Ye with the halcyons flitting delightedly
 Over the surge of the infinite sea,
 Come to the great Revolution awaiting us,
 Hither, come hither, come hither to me.

 *(Now the CHORUS OF BIRDS begins to arrive. Some flutter
 in from one upstage promontory, others swoop in from another.
 They whirr down the formations, crossing one another in spec-
 tacular dance movement.)*

EPOPS. All the feathered airy nation--
 Birds of every size and station
 Come in a flurry, with a hurry-scurry--
EUELPIDES. How they thicken, how they muster!
PITHETAERUS. How they clutter, how they cluster!
EUELPIDES. How they ramble here and thither,

How they scramble altogether.
There's a marsh bird...
PITHETAERUS. ...a flamingo--
EUELPIDES. Thyme-finch...
PITHETAERUS. ...ring-dove next, and then
Rock-dove, stock-dove,
cuckoo, falcon,
Fiery crest and willow wren.
EUELPIDES. Oho for the birds, oho, oho!
Oho for the blackbirds, ho!
CHORUS *(in final ecstatic movement)*.
Toro, toro, toro, torotinx
Kikkabau! Kikkabau! Toro, toro, toro, toro lililinx!

(With the last phrase the CHORUS OF BIRDS suddenly becomes still, perching about the stage in a great arc facing Epops, R. PITHETAERUS and EUELPIDES are crouching on our side of a rock L of C. The CHORUS LEADER steps forward.)

LEADER. We have answered the call of the King of the Birds.
We await his pleasure and attend his words.
EPOPS. An envoy, queer and shrewd,
Begs to address the multitude
Submitting to their decision
A surprising proposition--
CHORUS *(chattily pleasant, among themselves)*.
News amazing! News auspicious! News delightful, we agree.
EPOPS. Birds... two men of subtlest genius
Have proposed a plan to me.
CHORUS *(suddenly ruffled, stirring)*.
Who? What? When?
LEADER *(sternly)*. Say that again.
EPOPS *(indicating PITHETAERUS and EUELPIDES who now make bold to arise from behind their rock and present themselves modestly)*.
Here, I say, have come two humans
Traveling to the birds from man;

And they bring with them the kernel
Of a most stupendous plan.

CHORUS *(aroused now; shocked, angry).*

You have made the greatest error, since our life up here
began!

EPOPS. Now, you must'n't be so nervous--

EUELPIDES *(a little worried).* Everybody's *nervous!*

CHORUS *(rising to full height, awesomely).*

Explain your conduct, if you can!

EPOPS *(patiently, indicating them).*

I've received two men--

(PITHETAERUS is about to step forward and introduce himself, grandly.)

CHORUS *(shrill, terrifying, ruffling feathers).*

Among us? Have you really, truly dared?

EPOPS. Yes, and I shall introduce them--

EUELPIDES *(trembling).*

I hate to say it, but I'm getting scared!

CHORUS *(a great blast).* Out! Out upon you!

(PITHETAERUS and EUELPIDES, shaken by the impact, scurry to extreme DR and take shelter behind a ledge, as the CHORUS OF BIRDS turns from EPOPS and gathers in quick, violent consultation at L.)

We are cheated and betrayed, we have suffered shame and
wrong!

Our comrade and our King, who has fed with us so long,

Has broken every oath, and his holy plighted troth,

And the old social customs of our clan!

He has led us unawares into wiles and into snares--

He has given us as prey, all helpless and forlorn

To those who were our foes from the time that they were
born,

To vile and abominable man!

LEADER *(rising high among the choral group).*

For the bird our Chief, hereafter he must answer to the state!

With respect to these intruders, I propose, without debate,

Bit by bit to tear and rend them--

(The CHORUS OF BIRDS begins to sharpen their claws and make greedy, slavering sounds.)

PITHETAERUS. Here's a horrid mess.

EUELPIDES. It's all your fault, your fault, you and your cleverness! Why didn't you leave me home?

PITHETAERUS. I wanted a companion.

EUELPIDES. Your companion is going to melt into tears.

PITHETAERUS. Don't be silly. How're you going to cry with your eyes pecked out? *(EUELPIDES begins to bawl, loudly.)*

CHORUS *(thunderously, a climax to Euelpides' cry)*. Form in rank! Form in rank! *(CHORUS OF BIRDS begins to take military formation at L.)*

Then move forward and outflank them.

Let us see them overpowered,

Hacked, demolished, and devoured!

(Despairing pantomime by PITHETAERUS and EUELPIDES.)

Both, both of them shall die

And their bodies shall supply

Rare, dainty morsels for our beaks--

Where's the Captain? What detains him?

We are ready to proceed!

On the right there, call the captain!

Let him form his troop and lead!

(The CAPTAIN, a very shabby-looking bird, hurries in and proceeds to meet troops at L.)

PITHETAERUS. He's a seedy looking Captain.

CAPTAIN *(glancing back, huffily)*. I was moulting. *(Gives signal to BIRDS, who drop to crouched formation as though ready to spring into air and fly directly at the humans across stage.)*

EUELPIDES *(as CAPTAIN pantomimes instructions to the crouched and waiting CHORUS OF BIRDS)*. They're coming! They're coming! *(Shakes hands with PITHETAERUS, quickly.)* Good-bye. *(Starts directly toward CHORUS OF BIRDS.)*

PITHETAERUS *(grabbing him)*. Where do you think you're going?

EUELPIDES. I'm going to give myself up.

PITHETAERUS *(shaking him and roaring)*. Stand up and fight! Here! *(Digs into their equipment and hands him a fork.)*

EUELPIDES. Somehow I'm not hungry.

PITHETAERUS. Use it for a sword!

EUELPIDES. No. When my eyes are pecked out, I won't be able to see who I'm stabbing. I might stab myself.

PITHETAERUS *(throwing him a stewpot)*. Here! Shield your eyes!

EUELPIDES *(delighted, trying it on)*. Oh, that's nice! Want a test match? *(Begins to feint at PITHETAERUS, who slaps him away and digs out a pot and a ladle for his own weapons. At the same time the CAPTAIN leaps back from his pantomimed instructions to the CHORUS OF BIRDS and shouts.)*

CAPTAIN. Ready, Birds! Present your beaks! In double time, charge and attack!

LEADER. Pounce upon them...

CAPTAIN. ...smash the potlid--

LEADER. Clapperclaw them...

CAPTAIN. ...tear and hack! *(The CHORUS OF BIRDS leaps and darts forward and there ensues a slashing duel between the CHORUS OF BIRDS and PITHETAERUS and EUELPIDES. The CHORUS OF BIRDS keeps up a great chattering racket throughout. Momentarily PITHETAERUS and EUELPIDES disappear in a melee of surrounding BIRDS, then appear dueling each other. Recognizing their mistake, they separate and take on half the CHORUS OF BIRDS each. The CHORUS OF BIRDS forces them back to the rock towers, PITHETAERUS at R and EUELPIDES at L. The two men climb their towers, dueling, the CHORUS OF BIRDS pursuing, clawing at them. When both are about to be overcome, EPOPS decides to reassert himself, takes C.)*

EPOPS. Cease! Most unworthy creatures, scandal of the feathered race;

  Must I see my friends and yours massacred before my face? *(The CHORUS OF BIRDS pausess where they are, but do not release their hold on the humans.)*

CAPTAIN. Friends? They're *men*. Men invented the slingshot.

EUELPIDES. I hope they'll mark my grave.

EPOPS. But they have abandoned other men, and come to give us advice.

LEADER. Take advice... from an enemy?

EPOPS. How else do you suppose men learned to build strong walls, and make new weapons - if not from their enemies? We always learn from the enemy.

LEADER. Who are these men?

CAPTAIN. Why have they come to us?

EPOPS. Because they love you, and wish to share your life - to dwell and remain with you always.

LEADER. Are they mad?

EPOPS. The sanest men in the world.

EUELPIDES *(signaling EPOPS with his finger)*. Don't overdo it.

LEADER. Clever men, eh?

EPOPS. Cleverness itself! Men of the world, cunning, ingenious, sly... *(Searching for a perfect phrase.)*

PITHETAERUS *(prompting in a loud whisper)*. Brave. Brave.

EPOPS. And brave. They have wonderful plans!

LEADER. Plans?

EPOPS. To make us the rulers of the universe! All power, above and below, shall be ours! *(Chattering noises among the CHORUS OF BIRDS to each other; LEADER listens and considers.)*

LEADER. Well. I should like to hear this.

PITHETAERUS *(confident now, adopting an attitude)*. Well. You won't hear it from me.

CHORUS. What's this? What's this?

PITHETAERUS *(moving away toward R, stubborn)*. Not a word. I'm a clam.

EUELPIDES *(helpless)*. He's changed his mind. He wants to be a clam.

EPOPS. You must speak!

PITHETAERUS *(turning, in full command)*. Not until we reach an agreement! No more pecking, no more clawing, no more biting! Is it agreed?

LEADER *(after a glance around at the CHORUS OF BIRDS, whose heads bob up and down in encouragement)*. It is agreed.

CHORUS. We swear it. *(Raising one wing each.)*

LEADER. You have my word. And if I break my word... *(Glancing directly out front.)* ...may the audience speak unkindly of me in the lobby.

PITHETAERUS. Very well.

LEADER *(coming directly downstage now and speaking confidentially to the audience)*. On the other hand, if I keep my word, mention my performance to your friends. *(Turns immediately and rejoins CHORUS OF BIRDS as EPOPS speaks.)*

EPOPS. Birds! Gather yourselves and listen! *(In a quick flurry the CHORUS OF BIRDS darts to seated positions at R extending to C, facing the rock tower at L. As they speak, PITHETAERUS mounts the tower slowly.)*

CHORUS. Full of wiles, full of guiles, at all times, in all ways
Are the children of men. Still... we'll hear what he says.

EPOPS *(to PITHETAERUS)*. Speak!

PITHETAERUS *(surveys the group with slow deliberation, waiting for absolute silence; finally he speaks softly, for impressive effect)*. I am bursting to speak. *(Pause while he straightens to full height.)* I have already mixed the dough of my address and I am ready to knead it. *(Flurry of wings from the CHORUS OF BIRDS as though in applause.)*

EUELPIDES. A very pretty image.

PITHETAERUS *(takes a deep breath, begins to open his mouth and raise his arm in gesture; then halts)*. Water, please.

EUELPIDES. These long pauses are hard on the throat. *(LEADER scurries to the tower, taps a rock nearby and water gushes forth. PITHETAERUS drinks, wipes his mouth, faces his assembly again.)*

PITHETAERUS. I shall say what I have to say in a few, well-chosen words. *(EUELPIDES yawns loudly; PITHETAERUS hurls a rock at him; EUELPIDES ducks.)* Birds. My heart bleeds for you. You... who were formerly Emperors!

A BIRD *(to another near him, chattily)*. Did you ever hear that?

LEADER. Emperors? Over whom?

PITHETAERUS. Over all that exists! Over me. Over that man. *(Indicates EUELPIDES, who rises and bows.)* Over Zeus himself! You belong to a race older than Saturn - older than the Titans - older than the very Earth! *(EUELPIDES applauds, vociferously; PITHETAERUS throws another rock at him.)*

CHORUS. Than the Earth itself! We never heard that before.

PITHETAERUS *(warmed up now, the thoroughgoing demagogue)*. You never heard that before because you haven't read your Aesop! Aesop clearly tells us - and I quote -

that the lark - and the lark is a bird - existed before the Earth itself! *(Having reached a climax, he turns to drink.)*

EUELPIDES *(the unwelcome question)*. Where does Aesop say that?

PITHETAERUS *(stares at him hard, then dismisses it, speaking with casual rapidity as he takes up a cup and prepares to get more water)*. Oh, in that little story about how the lark's father died and went unburied for five days, and finally had to be buried in the lark's head. You know that.

EUELPIDES. No. I didn't. Now that I do, it doesn't seem to explain anything.

PITHETAERUS *(hurling the cup at him in sudden fury and then plunging directly into his speech)*. It explains this: if the lark had to bury its own father in its own head, that can only have been because there was no earth in which to bury him. Ergo, the lark existed before the Earth. Aesop. *(Pronounces his source with finality; the CHORUS OF BIRDS buzzes excitedly among themselves.)* Furthermore. The birds existed before the gods!

A BIRD *(to another, chattily)*. Do you think he's going too far?

PITHETAERUS *(thundering)*. The gods stole their power from the birds!

ANOTHER BIRD *(replying confidentially to the first)*. Too far.

PITHETAERUS. They derive their very authority from the birds! Else why should they carry on their sceptres - the symbol of their authority - a hawk? Why should Zeus always be seen with an eagle on his head?

LEADER *(interested)*. Why, indeed?

EUELPIDES. And so uncomfortable, too.

PITHETAERUS. Why should Victory be winged? Why Cupid? And, my friends, I ask you to consider the rooster.

EUELPIDES *(willing)*. All right.

PITHETAERUS. Just consider the rooster.

EUELPIDES. All right.

PITHETAERUS *(after a quick, disgusted glance at EUELPIDES)*. What creature, in all the universe, wears a crown that will not come off?

EUELPIDES *(after a moment's consideration)*. The rooster.

PITHETAERUS *(To EUELPIDES, annoyed)*. That was a rhetorical question.

EUELPIDES. That was a rhetorical answer.

PITHETAERUS *(whipping back into his tirade)*. All other crowns must be put on and taken off. Only a bird has a natural crown! Consider further. This Great King of old, this rooster, even now is so powerful, so great, so feared by men that the moment he crows at daybreak, they all jump out of bed. *(Pause for effect.)* What effect does the call of the rooster have?

EUELPIDES. Scares the hell out of me.

PITHETAERUS. It makes blacksmiths, potters, tanners, shoemakers, corn-dealers, lyre-makers, and amorers all put on their shoes and go to work even before it is daylight! This is the power of the bird! *(Quick change to pathos.)* And yet... how are birds treated today? Stones are thrown at you. Men set snares for you - twigs and nets of all kinds. You are caught. Caught. Sold in heaps for a banquet. The buyer fingers you over to be sure you are fat enough. *(CHORUS OF BIRDS shudders, emits little cries as PITHETAERUS pictures the full horror of their existence in juicy tones.)* If only... if only they would serve you up simply roasted. But no! What do they do? They grate cheese into a mixture of oil and vinegar - they add to this a greasy sauce - and they pour it scalding over your backs for all the world as though you were diseased meat! Oh! *(He cries out, unable to bear it; the CHORUS OF BIRDS echos him, takes up his wail.)*

CHORUS. Oh! Oh!
Sad and dismal is the story
We have heard this stranger tell
Of our fathers' ancient glory
Ere the fated empire fell.
(On their knees to PITHETAERUS.)
From the depths of degradation
A benignant happy fate
Sends you to restore our nation,
To redeem and save our state!

PITHETAERUS. Birds! The hour has come! Your power must be reclaimed - from men, and from the gods above!

EUELPIDES *(frowning)*. I just can't see Zeus turning things
  over to a woodpecker.
LEADER. But how shall we do this?
CHORUS. Tell us how!
PITHETAERUS *(during this he descends slowly and actually
  mingles with the CHORUS OF BIRDS, dramatizing it for them
  in gestures and whipping up their enthusiasm)*. Very well.
  First I propose that the Air you enclose
  And the space twixt the Earth and the Sky,
  Encircling it all with a brick-built wall
  Like Babylon's, solid and high.
  As soon as the building is brought to an end
  A herald or envoy to Zeus we shall send
  To require his immediate and prompt abdication;
  If he refuses, or shows hesitation
  Or evades the demand, we shall further proceed
  With legitimate warfare, avowed and decreed:
  (In the manner of a proclamation.)
  "Hereafter no god, neither Zeus nor any of the others resid-
  ing in heaven, may pass through our aerial domain for the
  purpose of impromptu love-making down below. Permission
  must first be granted by the Birds, and a small fee paid.
  Otherwise... back to Olympus!"
  *(CHORUS OF BIRDS chatters approval; he resumes his
  description.)*
  Another ambassador also will go
  To the Earth, and tell those below
  That in future:
  (Again the style of proclamation.)
  "Every man wishing to beg favors of the gods, and therefore
  offering sacrifice to the aforesaid gods, must first of all make
  an appropriate sacrifice to the Birds. For instance, if an ox is
  to be sacrificed to Zeus, the Birds must first be appeased by
  the sacrifice of one male mosquito!"
  (CHORUS OF BIRDS licks their chops in anticipation.)
LEADER. And what if they will not obey?
EUELPIDES. What if Zeus lets loose with thunder and light-
  ning?
LEADER. What if men ignore us?

PITHETAERUS. Then you will swoop onto their fields and eat up all their seed. *(EUELPIDES pantomimes this helpfully.)* Nothing will grow. Nor will Zeus be offered any oxen. You will fly to the pastures and peck out their eyes.

LEADER. And if they obey us, what do we promise in return?

PITHETAERUS. To defend their fields from insects and pests, as Zeus never did. Nevermore will they fear the beetle or roach. You will guide their sailing vessels, flying back to warn of an oncoming storm, and showing them favorable winds.

EUELPIDES *(starting to go)*. I'm leaving. I'm going into the shipping business. *(PITHETAERUS collars him, holds him steady, as the CHORUS OF BIRDS rises and then kneels in homage, with a burst of triumphant confidence.)*

CHORUS. All honor to you, oh man!
(PITHETAERUS takes a self-satisfied stance, and EUEL-PIDES leaps to the fore to share in the praise.)
We thought thee at first of our foemen the worst
And lo! we have found thee the wisest
And best of our friends. Our nation intends
To do whatsoever this great man advisest.
A spirit so lofty and rare
Thy words have within us excited
That we lift up our souls and we swear
That if thou wilt with us be united
In bonds that are holy and true
And honest and just and sincere--
If our hearts are attuned to one song,
We will march on the gods without fear!
Now whatever by muscle and strength can be done,
We birds will assuredly do;
But whatever by prudence and skill must be won,
We leave altogether to you.

EPOPS *(to PITHETAERUS)*. Come. Come with me and we shall lay our plans.

PITHETAERUS. Very well. *(To EUELPIDES, who has started off with EPOPS too willingly.)* Bring the luggage. *(EUEL-PIDES wearily goes back for their belongings and drags them forward. Meanwhile EPOPS has leaped to a great promontory as though to fly off when PITHETAERUS intervenes.)* Hi!

Wait! Come back here! How are we going to keep up with you? We haven't got wings.

EPOPS *(considering)*. That's true.

EUELPIDES *(tugging at Pithetaerus' sleeve, confidentially)*. I remember something else from Aesop. When the fox made an alliance with the eagle, he got the worst of it. *(PITHETAERUS pushes him away and his load throws him off balance.)*

EPOPS. Never fear. You shall eat of a certain root, and wings will grow on your shoulders.

LEADER *(to EPOPS)*. As you take them to dine, send us Procne. We wish to sing of our newfound happiness.

EPOPS *(turns on promontory and chants)*. Procne! Nightingale! Come forth!

(PROCNE darts onto stage from between rocks at UL.)

LEADER. Oh, nightingale - who are all melody - help us to show our joy! *(PROCNE dances to C.)*

EUELPIDES *(as PITHETAERUS follows EPOPS off L, dragging after them and looking back at PROCNE)*. Oh, that nice nightingale!

(PITHETAERUS reappears to collar him.)

EUELPIDES. How I should like to kiss her!

PITHETAERUS. You fool. She has two sharp points on her beak.

EUELPIDES *(sighing, lovelorn)*. I've got around worse. *(PITHETAERUS pulls him off with a great jerk, L. Only PROCNE and the CHORUS OF BIRDS, with their LEADER, are left. They now dance the following passage as they speak or sing it:)*

CHORUS *(addressing PROCNE, who dances)*.
Oh darling, oh tawny-throat!
Love, whom I love the best,
Dearer than all the rest.
Playmate and partner in all my soft lays,
Thou art come! Thou art come!

Thou art sweet to my gaze

And sweeter thy note... nightingale, nightingale!

PROCNE. Oh woodland muse--

CHORUS. Tio, tio, tio, tiotinx!

PROCNE. Of varied plume, with whose dear aid

On the mountain top, and the sylvan glade--

CHORUS. Tio, tio, tio, tiotinx!

PROCNE. I, sitting aloft on a leafy ash, full oft--

CHORUS. Tio, tio, tio, tiotinx!

PROCNE. Pour forth a warbling note from my little tawny throat,

Pour festive choral dances to the mountain mother's praise,

And to Pan the holy music of his own immortal lays,

CHORUS. Totototototototototinx,

Tio, tio, tio, tio, tiotinx!

PROCNE (*moving down toward the audience and speaking softly to it*).

You men who are dimly existing below,

Who perish and fade as the leaf--

Pale, woebegone, shadowlike, spiritless--

Frail castings in clay who are gone in a day

Like a dream full of sorrow and sighing,

Come listen with care to the birds of the air,

The ageless, the deathless, who flying

In joy and the freshness of air, are wont

To muse on wisdom undying.

CHORUS (*all speaking to the audience*).

Yes, take us for gods, as is proper and fit,

And Muses prophetic you'll have at your call,

Spring, winter, summer, and autumn and all.

And we won't run away from your worship and sit

Up above in the clouds, very stately and grand,

The way that old Zeus does. But, always at hand,

Health and wealth we'll bestow, as the formula runs,

On yourselves and your sons and the sons of your sons.

And happiness, plenty, and peace shall belong

To you all, and the revel, the dance, and the song

And laughter, and youth, we'll supply.

We'll never forsake you.

ONE BIRD *(a trifle giddy with it all)*. You'll be quite overburdened with pleasures and joys!

CHORUS. So happy and blest we will make you.

LEADER. Is there anyone amongst you, O spectators, who would lead

With the birds a life of pleasure?

CAPTAIN. Let him come to us with speed!

CHORUS. Truly to be clad in feather is the very best of things.
(With increasing lightness as they continue to face the audience but move to exit positions.)

Only fancy, dear spectators, had you each a brace of wings,

Never need you, tired and hungry, at our lengthy chorus stay.

You would lightly, when we bored you, spread your wings and fly away!

Back returning, after luncheon, to enjoy our comic play.

(CHORUS OF BIRDS disappears, slipping away behind various sections of rock. A moment later PITHETAERUS and EUELPIDES enter from UL, now equipped with great flopping wings which they are unable to manage properly. They test them awkwardly, absorbed, finally managing to bang them into one another. With this, PITHETAERUS pauses and really looks at EUELPIDES. He bursts out laughing.)

EUELPIDES. What are you laughing at?

PITHETAERUS. You. You look like a goose in a paint-bucket.

EUELPIDES. You look like a blackbird in need of a shave.

PITHETAERUS. Just think. They're our feathers. All our own.

EUELPIDES. D'you suppose we can fly?

PITHETAERUS *(pointing to a high rock)*. Go up there and jump off.

EUELPIDES *(sizing it up skeptically)*. No, I think I have a loose feather back here. *(Turning around and backing into PITHETAERUS.)* Would you see if I have a loose feather?

PITHETAERUS *(roaring)*. Would you get that thing out of my eye? *(In trying to disentangle himself from one of Euelpides' wings, he becomes enmeshed in the other and as EUELPIDES starts to turn around there is a pantomimed melee in which each fights his way through the other's wings. This concludes with PITHETAERUS booting EUELPIDES clear across the stage.)*

EUELPIDES *(looking up from his prone position on the ground).* Did I fly?

(EPOPS appears.)

PITHETAERUS. Hi, King-o! Look. The wings are very nice. But how do we fly?

EPOPS. You must go slowly at first, like the newborn bird fresh from the egg. One step at a time. *(EPOPS does one, to show them how. PITHETAERUS does his best to imitate it. EUEL-PIDES does a very cautious one, barely taking himself off the ground.)* Now another. *(They try again.)* And another. *(There ensues a dance in which EPOPS leads the two men in a series of leaps and bounds, he expertly, they clumsily. At conclusion:)* That will be enough for today.

EUELPIDES. Same time tomorrow?

PITHETAERUS. Now. We have work to do.

EPOPS. What first?

PITHETAERUS. Have the birds begun the city?

EPOPS. They are already hard at work. *(We hear sounds of hammering and building offstage.)* You hear?

(Several BIRDS cross through carrying sticks and straw.)

EPOPS. You see?

(During remainder of scene occasional BIRDS go through in this manner.)

PITHETAERUS. Then we must give our city a name.

EUELPIDES. Yes. We must have an address.

EPOPS. What shall we call it?

EUELPIDES. How about The New Athens?

PITHETAERUS. Not a word about Athens, city of pests!

EUELPIDES. How about Athens-on-the-Incline?

PITHETAERUS. Quiet!

EUELPIDES. How about Sparta?

PITHETAERUS. You! Into the air with you. Help the workers who are building the wall. Carry up rubble. Strip yourself to mix the mortar. Take up the hod. Tumble down the ladder. Post sentinels. *(EUELPIDES has started in a different direction with each command, and is now turning every way in a daze.)* Keep the fires burning! Go round the walls. Ring bells. Dispatch two heralds. One to the gods above. The other to mankind. And don't stop till you're finished!

(EUELPIDES finally falls out of sight beyond some rocks. At intervals during the following dialog he reappears, rushing messengers in various directions, pushing BIRDS carrying hods, etc.)

PITHETAERUS *(turning to EPOPS)*. Now. Do you have a priest-bird? To offer sacrifice.
EPOPS. Surely we're not going to offer sacrifice to the gods! We've just declared war!
PITHETAERUS. To the bird-gods... the new gods!
EPOPS. Ah! I will call him. *(EPOPS leaps to a high rock and emits a bird call to summon the PRIEST-BIRD. Then he whirls round to PITHETAERUS.)* But how can we offer sacrifice when we haven't named the city?
PITHETAERUS. I have named it.
EPOPS. You have a name?
PITHETAERUS. Just thought of it.
EPOPS. What? What is the name?
PITHETAERUS. Cloud Cuckoo-land!
EPOPS *(ravished)*. Cloud Cuckoo-land! Brilliant! Brilliant!

(To PRIEST-BIRD, as he enters.)

EPOPS. Here! Do as he tells you! *(To PITHETAERUS.)* I shall announce to the others our glorious name! *(EPOPS exits, as PITHETAERUS turns to PRIEST-BIRD.)*
PITHETAERUS. You are a priest-bird?
PRIEST. As my father before me, and his father before him, and his father before... *(This may go on forever.)*
PITHETAERUS. All right, all right. Do you know how to offer sacrifice?

PRIEST *(says nothing but immediately crosses to C, kneels, throws back his wings)*. I begin. *(Throws open his arms, then stops.)* Where's the sacrifice?

PITHETAERUS. Oh. *(He looks around, goes through the business of spotting a gnat flying through the air, pursuing and catching it; he then delicately deposits it before the PRIEST.)*

PRIEST *(peers at gnat dubiously, shrugs, and raises his arms again)*. Oh, birds who preside over the earth, and oh, god and goddess birds who preside over heaven--

PITHETAERUS *(getting into the act, kneeling down)*. Oh, hawk - oh, god of the storks!

PRIEST *(after a disdainful glance at PITHETAERUS, forces himself to continue, more fulsome)*. Oh, swan of Delos, oh, mother of the quails, oh, goldfinch--

PITHETAERUS. Goldfinch?

PRIEST *(paying no attention)*. Oh, ostrich, mother of the gods and mankind--

PITHETAERUS *(going along with it)*. Oh, ostrich--

PRIEST. Grant health and safety to the Cloud Cuckoo-landers, as well as to all who pay us tribute--

PITHETAERUS. Yes, put them in.

PRIEST. Oh, heroes - oh, sons of heroes - oh, sons of the sons of...

PITHETAERUS *(quickly)*. Don't get off on that again.

PRIEST. Oh, porphyrion--

PITHETAERUS *(competing with him now)*. Oh, pelican--

PRIEST. Oh, spoonbill--

PITHETAERUS. Oh--

PRIEST *(before PITHETAERUS can get one in)*. Oh, redbreast--

PITHETAERUS. Oh--

PRIEST *(beating him to it again)*. Oh, grouse-- *(Hereafter intoning more rapidly so that PITHETAERUS cannot do much more than get his mouth open for each phrase; PITHETAERUS becomes increasingly disgusted.)* Oh, peacock-- oh, horned-owl-- oh, heron-- oh, stormy petrel-- oh, woodpecker-- oh, titmouse--

PITHETAERUS. Oh, hell. *(Jumping up.)* That'll be enough now. Out of here, out of here. You'll drive me crazy. Next you'll be inviting the vultures. Can't you see there isn't enough sacrifice for more than one small bluebird? Out, out, I'll finish it myself.

(As he is hustling the PRIEST-BIRD off the stage, EUELPIDES is making the last of his flying trips through, urging a BIRD before him. PITHETAERUS grabs him and drags him downstage to position for sacrifice, as the BIRD scurries off.)

PITHETAERUS. Here. Don't say anything. Just assist me. *(PITHETAERUS gets down on his knees again, EUELPIDES mimics him, puzzled. PITHETAERUS spreads his arms.)* We will address our sacrifice to *all* winged things--

(Climbing up from the Earth below, a POET appears.)

POET. Hello! Anyone here?

EUELPIDES *(in an "oh-oh" tone of voice)*. Here comes the first pest.

POET *(in over-ecstatic admiration of the view)*. Oh, Muse! Oh, come, my Muse! Teach me to sing of happy, happy Cloud Cuckoo-land!

PITHETAERUS. What have we got here? Where'd you come from? Who are you?

POET. I am, a poet - a warbler - whose language is sweeter than honey. An eager, meagre servant of the Muses. As Homer says.

PITHETAERUS. You certainly wear your hair long!

POET. It flows as my songs do. Ah, I have worn myself out in the service of the Muses. As Homer says.

PITHETAERUS. Worn your cloak out, too, I see. What ill wind blew you up here?

POET *(taking out a great sheaf of papers)*. I have heard of your city, and I have composed a few small verses in its honor. They are small, but splendid.

PITHETAERUS. I see. And when did you compose them? How long since?

POET. Oh, I've been working at them a long time. Yes, a long, long time.

PITHETAERUS. That's interesting, considering I've just
founded the place. Just named it, like a little baby, two
minutes ago.

POET. Ah, but you reckon without the Muses, and how quickly
they spread the word!
(Declamatory.)
"Fleet, fleet as twinkling horses' feet
The airy, fairy rumor of the Muses.
Sped to me."
(Dropping tone.)
I went right to work.

PITHETAERUS. And why did you put yourself to such trouble?

POET. For beauty's sake. Beauty alone. The soul. *(Putting out
his hand, with pretended indifference.)* Of course, if you want
to give me a little something to keep body and soul together--

PITHETAERUS. As Homer says.

POET. Yes. I find it a little chilly walking the mountains in
these old things-- *(Indicating his ragged clothes and bravely
smiling. Then, by way of suggestion, his teeth begin to chatter.)*

EUELPIDES. Poor fellow. give him something.

PITHETAERUS. You think we ought to be charitable, do you?

EUELPIDES *(nodding)*. The generous man shares his benefits.

PITHETAERUS *(putting his arm around EUELPIDES)*. I have
misjudged you. You have a kind heart. *(Rips Euelpides' fur
jacket off and presents it to the POET.)* Here. Take this fur.
Maybe your teeth won't chatter so much.

POET. My Muse thanks you.

PITHETAERUS. It was nothing.

EUELPIDES. It was a fur jacket. *(Euelpides' teeth start to chatter.)*

POET. Do you remember those lovely lines from Pindar?

PITHETAERUS. Which ones?

POET. "Out among the Scythians yonder
See poor Straton wander, wander--
Poor, poor Straton, not possessed
Of a warmly woven under-vest.
What matter his jacket of fur if below
There's no soft tunic for him to show?

(Quietly.) Get it? *(PITHETAERUS starts toward EUEL-PIDES, as though to relieve him of something else - he hasn't much else on - but EUELPIDES backs away protesting.)*

EUELPIDES. I don't remember those lines! Don't remember 'em! *(But PITHETAERUS has snatched off another piece of Euelpides' clothing, leaving him in the absolute minimum.)*

PITHETAERUS *(tossing the garment to POET)*. Now here and get out. I can't spare another thing.

EUELPIDES. Not decently.

POET. I shall go, I shall go. And I shall sing your praises forever. *(Quoting, as he skips about the stage toward an exit.)*
"Oh, Muse, on your golden throne
Prepare me a solemn ditty.
To the mighty, to the flighty,
To the cloudy, quivering, shivering,
To the snowy, to the blowy lovely city.
Cloud Cuckoo-land! Cloud Cuckoo-land!
Tra la la la la la la la la!"
(POET has danced off.)

PITHETAERUS. What's he talking about - snowy, blowy? We gave him the clothes off our backs! How d'you suppose that plague found his way up here already? *(EUELPIDES is about to reply, but his chattering teeth prevent him.)* What are you muttering about? *(EUELPIDES tries helplessly to speak but again breaks down into chattering.)* Come, back to the sacrifice. And don't say a word. *(EUELPIDES motions that he can't, pointing to his chattering teeth; Pithetaerus' arms are spread again.)* Oh, snowbird! *(EUELPIDES worse than ever at this.)* Oh, penguin-- *(EUELPIDES shivering all over.)* Oh, gull of the frosty mountains--! *(EUELPIDES in a state of collapse.)*

(A PROPHET has climbed into view from the Earth below.)

PROPHET. Cease! Do not continue the sacrifice!
PITHETAERUS. Why not?
PROPHET. All the signs are against it!
PITHETAERUS. Who are you?
PROPHET. I... am a prophet, and the author of several prophetic books. *(The PROPHET might well speak in a voice*

resembling that of some contemporary radio or television oracle.)

PITHETAERUS. Beat it.

PROPHET. Fool! Would you fly in the face of destiny? There is a prophecy in my book... *(Opens a huge volume he carries.)* ...which applies exactly to Cloud Cuckoo-land.

PITHETAERUS. This is a fine time to tell me! Why didn't you mention it while I was on Earth below, before I got everything started?

PROPHET *(wisely)*. The time was not propitious. However, since hearing of the foundation of Cloud Cuckoo-land, Apollo has appeared to me in a dream. He has interpreted the prophecy in my book. Which I shall now interpret for you.

PITHETAERUS *(wearily)*. All right. Interpret.

PROPHET *(reading portentously)*. "When the wolves and the white crows shall dwell together between the spoon and the great bowl..."

PITHETAERUS. Now, see here. What has all this kitchenware got to do with me?

PROPHET. The great bowl stands for Cloud Cuckoo-land - when you know how to interpret it. It continues: "Before a sacrifice can be offered, those who would offer it must first give to the prophet who reveals these words, a new pair of sandals." *(EUELPIDES just sits down and takes off his shoes.)*

PITHETAERUS. It says sandals, does it?

PROPHET *(smugly)*. Look at the book. *(Reading again.)* "Besides this, he must be given a goblet of wine and a good share of the entrails of the victim sacrificed." *(EUELPIDES peers closely at the gnat, wondering how this is to be done.)*

PITHETAERUS. It says entrails, does it?

PROPHET. Look at the book. "If you do as I command, you shall be an eagle among the clouds. If not, you shall be neither turtle-dove, nor eagle, nor woodpecker."

PITHETAERUS. It says all that, does it?

PROPHET. Look at the book.

PITHETAERUS. You know, that's funny. Apollo appeared to me in a dream, too. He told me how to interpret another passage.

PROPHET. He did?

PITHETAERUS. Yes. *(Snatching the book.)* Ah, here it is. *(Obviously improvising.)* "If an impostor comes without invitation to annoy you during the sacrifice and to demand a share of the victim, give to this man a sharp blow on the head."

PROPHET. Ridiculous!

PITHETAERUS. Look at the book. *(Shoves the book under Prophet's nose. PROPHET incredulously peers at it, and PITHETAERUS claps it shut on his nose. As PROPHET dances away in pain, PITHETAERUS batters him with it soundly, driving him to a high rock from which he leaps; PITHETAERUS hurls the book down after him, and we hear a faraway howl.)*

EUELPIDES *(holding up his sandals)*. All right to put these back on?

PITHETAERUS *(dusting off his hands, coming down)*. Yes.

EUELPIDES. My Muse thanks you.

(EUELPIDES sneezes while putting them on and thereafter develops a cold, which affects his voice. Meantime, a REAL ESTATE MAN, equipped with curious measuring instruments, has climbed from the Earth below. PITHETAERUS lets out a mighty roar on seeing him, which frightens EUELPIDES.)

EUELPIDES. What? What?

PITHETAERUS. Another one!

REAL ESTATE MAN *(briskly and efficiently striding C with his instruments. See Production Notes.*)* Good morning. Good morning. Nice development you have here.

PITHETAERUS. What are you after? Who are you?

REAL ESTATE MAN. I am going to survey the plains of the air for you. Then we'll subdivide.

PITHETAERUS. What are those things?

REAL ESTATE MAN. Tools. For measuring the air.

PITHETAERUS. You can measure the air, can you?

REAL ESTATE MAN. Oh, yes. With this bent ruler I draw a line from top to bottom. From one of its points I describe a circle with the compass. Then I take the hypotenuse. Follow me?

PITHETAERUS. Not at all.

REAL ESTATE MAN (*patronizing throughout*). Well, we can't all understand these things. Next, with a straight ruler I inscribe a square within the circle. Its center will be the marketplace, into which all the straight streets will lead. They will converge to a center like a star, which, although only orbicular, sends forth its rays in a straight line from all sides. Better now?

PITHETAERUS. Come here. I want to talk with you. (*Draws him downstage, confidentially.*)

REAL ESTATE MAN (*beaming*). Yes?

PITHETAERUS. You don't know this, but I'm a friend of yours.

REAL ESTATE MAN. Oh, that's nice.

PITHETAERUS. Don't let on, but I'm going to slip you a piece of advice.

REAL ESTATE MAN. Oh, fine. What's that?

PITHETAERUS. Run. Run like hell.

REAL ESTATE MAN. Good heavens! Have I an enemy here?

PITHETAERUS. Yes.

REAL ESTATE MAN. Someone in the city?

PITHETAERUS. Yes. Someone very important. In fact, he's had a law passed.

REAL ESTATE MAN. What's that?

PITHETAERUS. "All quacks, profiteers, and other pests are to be swept from the borders."

REAL ESTATE MAN (*thinking it over a moment*). Oh. Then *I'd* better be going. (*Starts, hesitates.*) Tell me one thing. Who is this person I have to fear?

PITHETAERUS (*beckons to him, very confidential, heads together*). Me.

REAL ESTATE MAN. Oh, I see! You're joking! (*Laughs heartily. PITHETAERUS joins in the laugh and, as though slapping him jovially, gives him a smart blow. REAL ESTATE MAN sobers at this.*) You *are* joking?

PITHETAERUS (*hitting him harder and laughing*). Yes, yes!

REAL ESTATE MAN (*reeling from blows, suspiciously*). You're *not* joking!

(*In a roar of laughter, PITHETAERUS pummels him severely, driving him across the stage. But before he can get him off, they*

*pass a TAX INSPECTOR who has just come up from Earth,
equipped with notebook and tax forms. PITHETAERUS
doubles back in a non-stop movement, grabbing the TAX IN-
SPECTOR by the seat of the pants.)*

PITHETAERUS. Here, now! This is the way out!
INSPECTOR *(routine formality)*. You will please declare your
   personal property.
PITHETAERUS. Who sent you?
INSPECTOR. Government. Tax inspector.
PITHETAERUS. Haven't got any personal property. We've just
   started to build.
INSPECTOR. Very well. I'll have to leave an estimated bill,
   based upon what we happen to need at the moment. *(Having
   scribbled on form, rips it off and hands it to PITHETAERUS.)*
PITHETAERUS *(tearing it up matter-of-factly)*. Very well. And
   I'm going to make an estimated payment, based upon how I
   happen to feel at the moment-- *(Hits him with a stewpot
   which EUELPIDES has casually handed him, then trips him
   up.)*
INSPECTOR. You'll go to court... you'll go to court!

   *(A LAWYER has arrived from Earth during this melee and is
   already tacking a list of printed regulations to a place on the
   rocks. PITHETAERUS sees him.)*

PITHETAERUS. Here! What are you putting up there?
LAWYER. The new laws for the community. "If a Cloud Cuck-
   oo-lander should commit libel against Athens or any
   Athenian..."
PITHETAERUS *(tearing down list to look at it)*. We don't need
   any lawyers up here!
LAWYER. Have to have lawyers. Don't want to spend all our
   time in jail, do we?
PITHETAERUS *(reading)*. "The Cloud Cuckoo-landers shall
   adopt the same weights and measures as now prevail in..."
LAWYER. The standard weights and measures, of course.
PITHETAERUS. No, we have new measures up here. Like this.
   (Pushes him backward over EUELPIDES, who has prepared

*himself. At same time LAWYER has pulled himself together
and from now on, both PITHETAERUS and EUELPIDES are
very busy handling the reappearing pests, no sooner laying
hands on one than another pops up, until the stage is a swirl of
confused activity.)*

INSPECTOR. You are now liable to penalty of ten thousand...

*(As PITHETAERUS is getting hold of him, POET has reap-
peared.)*

POET. Tralalalalalalalalala! My Muses are back. They say I
should also have a crown. *(EUELPIDES claps the stewpot
over his head.)*

LAWYER *(reading from list)*. "Should anyone drive away the
magistrates and not receive them, according to the decree
duly posted..."

EUELPIDES *(calling off to the BIRDS, desperate)*. Help! Help!
We have vermin!

(PROPHET has also reappeared.)

PROPHET. I came to tell you that your doom is sealed. I have
just had another chat with Apollo... *(PITHETAERUS and
EUELPIDES cannot keep up with all of them and are losing
the battle. The combined nuisances are surrounding them, suc-
cessfully bending their ears, forcing them into a tight knot DC.)*

REAL ESTATE MAN. What I forgot to mention is that there is
a great profit in this for you, personally--

INSPECTOR. Of course, if you would like to offer a small
bribe--

PROPHET. The signs are all very unfavorable--

*(PITHETAERUS and EUELPIDES slump exhausted DC, as
POET, PROPHET, REAL ESTATE MAN, TAX INSPEC-
TOR, and LAWYER bend over them, all talking at once, ad lib-
bing in a great yammering babble, PITHETAERUS and EUEL-
PIDES hold their ears, rocking back and forth. By this time
BIRDS have begun to appear over the rocks. Some of them, car-
rying a great net, steal downstage behind the group and, at a sig-*

*nal, throw the net over the yammering nuisances.
PITHETAERUS and EUELPIDES immediately duck out from
under and the net is drawn tight about the others.)*

PROPHET *(a continuation of his previous line, with net business
timed between).* I was so right.

POET. Whither has joy flown? Oh, darkest day!

INSPECTOR *(inside net).* Get me a lawyer!

LAWYER *(right next to him, inside net).* I'm a lawyer.

PITHETAERUS. There! Now we'll put them all in a man-cage.
We'll hang them from the ceiling of Cloud Cuckoo-land, and
there they can sing to us all day! Take them away!
*(PITHETAERUS and EUELPIDES supervise the BIRDS as
they drag them out of sight beyond rocks and the CHORUS OF
BIRDS takes over.)*

CHORUS *(a great burst).*
Hear ye!
Henceforth - our worth,
Our right, our might,
Shall be shown,
Acknowledged, known.
Mankind shall raise
Prayers, vows, praise
To the Birds alone!
(Change of tone, lighter.)
Oh, the happy clan of birds
Clad in feather,
Needing not a woolen vest in
Wintry weather--

*(PITHETAERUS and EUELPIDES return, dusting off their
hands. The CHORUS OF BIRDS are distributing themselves in
happy, comfortable, languorous positions, and PITHETAERUS
and EUELPIDES move DC, stretch out, entirely comfortable at
last. BIRDS bring them fruit and wine, drop grapes into their
mouths - in all, the picture of sybaritic luxury.)*

CHORUS. Heeding not the warm far-flashing
Summer ray,

For within the leafy bosoms
Of the flowery meads we stay,
When the Chirruper in ecstasy is shrilling forth his tune,
Maddened with the sunshine and the raptures of the noon.
And we winter in the caverns' hollow spaces.
In spring we crop the flowers of the myrtles white and tender,
Dainties that are fashioned in the gardens of the graces.
(Climax of luxurious passage.)
Oh, many a herb and many a berry
Serves to feast and make us merry! *(Pause.)*
It's a nice life.
(Real break from choral quality to conversational prose tone.)
And now, just before the intermission, one word to the
critics. If the reviews are good tomorrow, we are prepared to
do several nice things for you. We will build nests in your
chimneys and sing for you sweetly from time to time. When
we die, we will leave you our claws, for use on other oc-
casions. As you sit down to dinner, we may even fly in with
some plovers' eggs, if you happen to like them. *(Slight pause.)*
On the other hand, should the reviews be bad tomorrow -
and should the critics thereafter just happen to be walking
down a public street - well, let them wear hats. *(Portentous,
with a slight upward glance.)* Let *them wear hats!*

CURTAIN

End of Act One

ACT TWO

SCENE: *As before. PITHETAERUS discovered asleep on the stage. He wakes up, stretches, yawns, then gets up, pleasantly drowsy. He comes directly downstage and speaks in an easy conversational tone.*

PITHETAERUS *(to audience).* Well, friends. We've got the sacrifice over with and those pests out of the way. So far, so good. Now we'll have to make preparations for a splendid banquet to celebrate the building of the city. Just as soon as it's built. That reminds me. I haven't had any report on how it's coming. There ought to be a messenger, bringing me news. There always is a messenger in these plays. It's not right to have no messenger. Probably produced this thing on a low budget. Still, maybe one will be coming along. We'll have to look. *(Goes to high point, looks off.)* Ah, yes. Swift as lightning, he comes!

(As PITHETAERUS turns to greet him, the FIRST MESSENGER speeds in at a terrific rate, passing PITHETAERUS altogether and exiting opposite. PITHETAERUS looks after him, pokes his way down near where FIRST MESSENGER has gone off. At this moment FIRST MESSENGER whizzes past him again from opposite direction, and off. PITHETAERUS has nearly had his nose clipped off in the process. He now considers a moment, starts toward second exit, but pauses a moment to pick up a rock and weigh it in his hand, then climbs to a point above exit prepared to drop rock on returning First Messenger's head. FIRST MESSENGER whizzes in again, PITHETAERUS hurls the rock down onto his own foot. His yowl stops the FIRST MESSENGER, who turns, but who continues his running motions even as he speaks.)

45

FIRST MESSENGER. Where is he? Where, where? Oh, where? Where is he?

PITHETAERUS. Who, dammit?

FIRST MESSENGER. Our leader, Pithetaerus. Where is he?

PITHETAERUS. Here, you idiot! *(Grabs him to stop his legs from running motions.)*

FIRST MESSENGER *(stepping back, military, breathing hard)*. You... are... Pithetaerus?

PITHETAERUS. Yes, dammit!

FIRST MESSENGER *(a military step forward, with a salute, still breathing hard)*. I have a message for you, sir.

PITHETAERUS. That's what I thought. Well, well, what is it? *(FIRST MESSENGER opens mouth to deliver message, then faints dead away on the floor.)* Oh, these bit players! Here! Here! Come to! *(Slapping him vigorously. FIRST MESSENGER comes to, dazed, and PITHETAERUS lifts him to his feet. FIRST MESSENGER immediately begins running again.)* Here, stop! *(Grabs FIRST MESSENGER.)* Now. What's the message?

FIRST MESSENGER. The wall is finished.

PITHETAERUS *(dismissing him, as though finished)*. Good.

FIRST MESSENGER *(holding his ground)*. And a most amazing, magnificent work it is!

PITHETAERUS *(turning back, a gesture of dismissal)*. Fine, fine.

FIRST MESSENGER *(obviously has a set-speech of a part and is going to deliver it, no matter what)*. Big enough for two chariots to pass on it, driven by steeds as big as the Trojan horse. *(Becoming increasingly declamatory, with gestures.)*

PITHETAERUS. That's wonderful. Good-bye.

FIRST MESSENGER. The height - I measured it myself - is exactly a hundred fathoms.

PITHETAERUS *(being drawn into it now)*. Is that so? Who could have built such a wall?

FIRST MESSENGER *(making the most of his opportunity, taking over the stage, walking away from PITHETAERUS toward audience)*. The Birds! Nobody else, no foreigners, Egyptian bricklayers, workmen or masons. But they themselves - alone - by their own efforts--

PITHETAERUS *(aware of what he is doing, mockingly helpful)*. Unaided.

FIRST MESSENGER *(striding off to another part of stage, forcing PITHETAERUS to follow him)*. The birds, I say, completed everything. I was as surprised as you are. But I was there. An eyewitness.

PITHETAERUS *(same tone, more mocking)*. You saw it.

FIRST MESSENGER *(striding off again)*. I saw it.
There came a body of thirty thousand cranes
With stones from Africa--
I won't be positive. There might have been more.

PITHETAERUS *(irritated, shouting, hoping he'll get on with it and get off)*. All right! There were more.

FIRST MESSENGER. With stones from Africa in their craws and gizzards,
Which the sandpipers and stone-chatterers
Worked into shape and finished.
The mudlarks, too, were busy in their department
Mixing the mortar, while the water birds
As fast as it was wanted, brought water
To temper and loosen it.

PITHETAERUS *(fascinated by his spiel)*. Who were the masons? Who did you get to carry it?

FIRST MESSENGER. Carry? Why, the carrion crows, of course. *(Laughs loudly at the audience, announcing this as a joke. PITHETAERUS hits him a quieting slap.)*

PITHETAERUS. I'll tell the jokes. How did you fill the hods? How did they manage that?

FIRST MESSENGER. Oh, capitally, I promise you! *(Demonstrating the following movements ludicrously with his hands and feet.)*
There were the geese, all barefoot,
Trampling the mortar, and when all was ready
They handed it into the hods... so cleverly--
With their flat feet!
(He is making a production number out of this. PITHETAERUS says nothing so he repeats the business without the lines.)

PITHETAERUS. All right, you do that very well. Go on.

FIRST MESSENGER. You should have been there. It was a sight to see them.

Trains of ducks, clambering the ladders--

(Demonstrating again.)

With their little duck legs, like bricklayer's prentices,

All dapper and handy, with their little trowels.

(Shows how they trowel with their beaks.)

PITHETAERUS *(nailing him down)*. Could you finish this standing still? What of the woodwork? Who were the carpenters?

FIRST MESSENGER. The woodpeckers, of course! And there they were

Laboring upon the gates, driving and banging

With their hard hatchet beaks, and such a din,

Such a clatter as they made, hammering and hacking,

In a perpetual peal, pelting away,

Like shipwrights, hard at work in the docks.

PITHETAERUS. You had a lot to say once you got started, didn't you?

FIRST MESSENGER *(exuberantly, for climactic effect)*.

And now their work is finished, gates and all,

Staples and bolts, and bars and everything.

The sentries at their posts, patrols appointed,

Watchmen in the towers, the beacons

Prepared for lightning, all their signals set--

(Immediate drop to conversational tone.)

And now if you'll excuse me, I have to wash my hands.

(Drops off the stage and goes up the aisle of the theatre to the men's washroom. At same time EPOPS and the CHORUS OF BIRDS begin to appear over the rocks.)

EPOPS. Well! What do you say to us? Aren't you astonished at how quick we've been? The city completed and ready?

PITHETAERUS. By the gods, yes. It's simply not to be believed. *(A stir is heard offstage.)* What's that?

LEADER. A messenger is coming.

PITHETAERUS. Not another! Well, somebody's got to help me this time!

(SECOND MESSENGER darts in, as first one did. PITHETAERUS immediately blocks off second exit, causing SECOND MESSENGER to turn and head for another, but the CHORUS OF BIRDS leaps to positions blocking him off one place and another until he is surrounded and crowded in DC, still running in a static position, facing front. On a signal, PITHETAERUS and surrounding CHORUS OF BIRDS grabs him to stop him.)

SECOND MESSENGER. Alas, alas, alas, alas, alas!
PITHETAERUS. Is that the whole message?
SECOND MESSENGER. Terrible news!
CHORUS. What? What news? What's the matter?
PITHETAERUS *(to CHORUS OF BIRDS)*. Sh-h-h! Be quiet! *(In shushing them, PITHETAERUS has momentarily loosed his hold on SECOND MESSENGER, who promptly starts running again. PITHETAERUS tackles him in a flying dive. SECOND MESSENGER goes down and out. PITHETAERUS is bending over him.)* What news? *(No response from SECOND MESSENGER.)* Now he's out. Here! Here! Answer me!

(Begins the slapping business. At same time a rope dangles down from the city above and, as CHORUS OF BIRDS clears a space, EUELPIDES slides down it.)

EUELPIDES. Ho, there! Look out below!
PITHETAERUS. What are you doing?
EPOPS. He's come from the city.
EUELPIDES. I still don't trust these wings.
PITHETAERUS. Get down out of there!
EUELPIDES. Did you get the message?
PITHETAERUS. No, dammit! *(To EPOPS, as he glances at knocked-out SECOND MESSENGER.)* Put it on order right away - stronger messengers!
LEADER. Tell us! What is this terrible news?
EUELPIDES *(dropping to the stage floor)*. A horrible outrage. Horrible!
PITHETAERUS. Well, get on with it!

EUELPIDES. Here's what happened-- *(The SECOND MES-SENGER has been coming to, unnoticed.)* The gods have heard about our intention, and Zeus has already...

SECOND MESSENGER *(quickly jumping in, attempting to give the message himself, overlapping EUELPIDES)*. The thing is that Zeus has already heard what we plan to do-- *(Both EUELPIDES and SECOND MESSENGER continue explaining but since they are both talking at once, we cannot understand a word they are saying.)*

PITHETAERUS. Silence! Shut up! One at a time!

EUELPIDES *(to SECOND MESSENGER, quarrelsome)*. You lie down.

SECOND MESSENGER. But I was sent here to...

EUELPIDES. *I* started to tell this story.

SECOND MESSENGER. I got here first!

EUELPIDES *(shouting)*. You had your chance! You didn't...

SECOND MESSENGER. But they're *my* lines!

EUELPIDES. I slid all the way down here, getting several rope burns-- *(By now they are shouting at each other at the same time and they begin to rough it up. PITHETAERUS pulls them apart.)*

PITHETAERUS. Here! Here!

SECOND MESSENGER. I was sent here to relay this information--

PITHETAERUS. Look. You've run a long way. Don't you want to wash your hands?

SECOND MESSENGER *(reflective pause)*. As a matter of fact, I do.

PITHETAERUS *(pointing down aisle to men's washroom)*. Right there.

SECOND MESSENGER. Oh. Thank you.

(Leaps offstage as FIRST MESSENGER has done; at same time FIRST MESSENGER reappears from men's washroom and they pass each other midway down the aisle, shake hands, and go their ways, SECOND MESSENGER to the men's washroom, FIRST MESSENGER up onto the stage.)

PITHETAERUS *(seeing FIRST MESSENGER coming)*. Now before *he* gets up here with *his* big mouth, will you tell us the news?

EUELPIDES. A god has penetrated the city.

CHORUS. What? A sacrilege, on the day our city was built! Oh, horrible! Let terror strike.

EUELPIDES *(shrugging his shoulders)*. Got through somehow.

LEADER. Who was on guard?

EUELPIDES. The jays.

LEADER. Death to the jays!

EUELPIDES. But it's one of those minor gods with little wings. That made it tougher.

EPOPS. Where is this god now?

EUELPIDES. We don't know. Flying around somewhere. Liable to turn up any minute.

PITHETAERUS *(to LEADER)*. Dispatch thirty thousand hawks of the Legion of Mounted Archers!

LEADER *(hustling some BIRDS off and calling offstage to others, bawling orders. A few BIRDS remain, gathered about EPOPS)*. All hook-clawed birds into the air! Kestrels, buzzards, vultures, great-horned owls! Cleave the air till it resounds with the flapping of wings. Look everywhere!

CHORUS. To arms, all, with beak and talon!

War, a terrible war, is breaking out between us and the gods!

LEADER. Look everywhere! *(A conventional puff of smoke at opposite side of stage.)*

EUELPIDES. Look right there.

(ALL huddle at opposite side, staring toward the rock from which the smoke puff has come. IRIS appears through the cloud, an unlikely looking goddess with small wings. She stands looking at them, then speaks in a flat, nasal voice.)

IRIS. Hello.

PITHETAERUS. Halt! Don't stir. Not a beat of your wing. Who are you? Where do you come from?

IRIS. Me? I come from Olympus, my abode.

PITHETAERUS. Who are you?

IRIS. I yam swift Iris.

PITHETAERUS. Call the buzzards and let them seize her!

IRIS. Say, I handled plenty of buzzards who tried to do that.

PITHETAERUS. Woe to you!

IRIS. Woe to you, too. What's up?

LEADER. By which gate did you pass through the wall, wretched goddess?

IRIS. I didn't see no gate. I was just out for a short flap.

PITHETAERUS. Fine, innocent airs she gives herself! *(Mockingly.)* You applied to the pelicans, I suppose? The captain of the cormorants let you in?

IRIS. Well, I seen a nice captain, but I let it pass.

PITHETAERUS. So, you confess! You came without permission! You didn't get a passport. Nobody put a label on you!

IRIS *(instinctively starts to reach with her hand, stops).* Is that what that was?

PITHETAERUS. Without permission from anybody, you ramble and fly through the air - the air that belongs to us!

IRIS. To you?

CHORUS. To us!

IRIS. Where do you think us gods are gonna take our exercise?

PITHETAERUS. I don't know and I don't care. But I'll tell you this - let us catch you once more flying through this territory and you're done for. You'll be put to death.

CHORUS. To death!

IRIS. Listen. I'm immortal.

PITHETAERUS. Don't try to wriggle out of it, now. Mortal or immortal, you'll be put to death. We can't have the whole universe obeying us and you lackadaisical gods floating around where you please.

IRIS *(snaps her fingers).* Almost forgot. Had an errand to do. *(Starts to promenade across the stage.)*

PITHETAERUS. Wait a minute, here! What errand?

IRIS. Zeus sent me. I'm supposed to go down to Earth and tell mankind to sacrifice an ox. Zeus wants a little heady smoke coming up. Helps his sinus.

PITHETAERUS. Sacrifice to him?

IRIS. Who else? Zeus, he's my father. He's a deity.

PITHETAERUS. Zeus a deity? *(Laughs mockingly. BIRDS join him in a great hollow cackling.)*

IRIS. Best deity going.

PITHETAERUS *(roaring)*. Silence! Remember - once and for all - that we, the birds, are the only deities, from this time forth!

IRIS. Huh?

PITHETAERUS. Man henceforth will sacrifice to us and not to Zeus, by Zeus!

IRIS *(suddenly going into grand tragic style, beating her breast, clinging dramatically to rocks, writhing on the floor, etc.)*.
Oh, fool, fool, fool! Stir not the mighty wrath
Of angry gods, lest Justice, with the spade
Of vengeful Jove, demolish all thy race,
And fiery vapor, with lightning strokes,
Incinerate thy city and thyself!

PITHETAERUS *(matter-of-fact tone)*. Now, listen, girl. Never mind the oratory. You can save that speech for some tragedy or other. And if Zeus keeps troubling me, I'll be doing some incinerating myself. *(Slowing down his rate, half-abstracted as he looks at her.)* I'll send eagles carrying fire up into his halls of state, and he'll find out. *(Slower still.)* And as for you, unless you learn to mind your manners-- *(Suddenly.)* Say, are you doing anything tonight?

IRIS *(backing away from him)*. I'll tell my father, I'll tell my father--

PITHETAERUS *(giving it up)*. Oh, bother. Scuttle away. Convey your person elsewhere. Be brisk. Leave a vacancy. Brush off. *(She has backed away but not gone. He shouts.)* Well?

IRIS *(terrified, as she runs off)*. Daddy! Zeus! Daddy!

CHORUS. Never again shall the Zeus-born gods
Never again shall they pass this way!
Never again through this realm of ours
Shall men send up to the heavenly powers
The smoke of beasts which on earth they slay!
We, too, shall slay! Slay!

PITHETAERUS. Now whatever's happened to that herald we sent down to Earth, to tell the people? *(To EUELPIDES.)* You sent him, didn't you?

EUELPIDES. I did.

PITHETAERUS. Why can't we keep these actors around here?

(HERALD enters on the double, late, obviously having missed his cue, and still fixing his costume.)

EUELPIDES. He's in.

HERALD *(stentorian tones)*. Oh, Pithetaerus!

PITHETAERUS. High time.

HERALD. Oh, thou wisest, thou best - oh, thou wisest *and* best - thou wisest, deepest, happiest of mankind - happiest, deepest, wisest--

PITHETAERUS. Did he play the priest in the first act?

HERALD. Most glorious Pithetaerus, most... *(Snapping his fingers, looking off.)* Prompter! Prompter!

PROMPTER'S VOICE *(off)*. Revered of men--

HERALD. Revered of men, most... *(Thinks a moment, then speaks confidentially to PITHETAERUS.)* Let me try it again. *(Takes a step back as though entering anew, begins from the beginning.)* Oh, Pithetaerus!

PITHETAERUS. No, you don't! Suppose we get on with the message?

HERALD *(hurt)*. All right. But I knew it. *(Stentorian again.)* All men on Earth have been notified, and all are filled with admiration for your wisdom. They acknowledge your leadership, and that of the Birds, and have sent you this golden crown. *(Holds out his hands in motion of giving crown, but they are empty.)*

PITHETAERUS. Yes?

HERALD *(noticing he has no crown)*. Oh, dammit! *(Goes to the wings.)* Where's that crown? Somebody was supposed to hand it to me!

PROMPTER'S VOICE *(off)*. You were supposed to pick it up!

HERALD *(shouting off, beginning an ad lib quarrel, both talking at once)*. When an actor has to make an entrance, he can't be worrying about props! *(There is an almost out-of-sight scuffle between the HERALD and some member of the stage crew, whose hands only are seen, over the crown. PITHETAERUS wearily breaks in, brings HERALD back to position, plants him there, thrusts the crown into his hands, deliberately takes it out again, doing the whole business himself to make sure it gets done, and crams it on his own head in disgust.)*

PITHETAERUS. Now will you get on with the message?

HERALD *(pulling himself together)*. All right. *(In a sudden confidence to PITHETAERUS.)* Do you get stage fright? I do.

PITHETAERUS *(roaring)*. Get on with it!

HERALD *(opens his mouth to speak, then breaks down completely, a nervous shambles)*. I'm sorry. I'll have to turn in my part. I'm a wreck. *(He leaves.)*

PITHETAERUS. Does anybody know his lines?

FIRST MESSENGER *(hopping to his feet)*. Yes, sir. I do!

PITHETAERUS. I'd hoped it would be anybody but you. All right.

FIRST MESSENGER *(quickly taking Herald's place)*. I, who have just returned from Earth... *(Aside to PITHETAERUS.)* I haven't, of course. I'm saying *his* lines. *(Back into speech.)* ...bring you this message. All men accept your reign and themselves wish to become birds. More than ten thousand have followed me here and now await your pleasure. They have gone bird-mad.

(HERALD sticks his head in from the wings.)

HERALD *(to FIRST MESSENGER)*. I hate you.

(PITHETAERUS makes a threatening gesture and HERALD disappears again. We begin to see the hands and heads of people climbing up from Earth. PITHETAERUS is immediately aware of them and he goes to the Earth-entrance and is busy counting heads as the FIRST MESSENGER completes his speech.)

FIRST MESSENGER. They wish to be supplied with feathers and hooked claws, in honor of their masters. Will you oblige them?

PITHETAERUS. Ah, yes. Yes, indeed. Quick! There's no time for idling.

(MEN enter, arriving from Earth.)

PITHETAERUS. Go and fill every hamper, every basket you
can find with wings. Bring them to me, and I will welcome
our new subjects!

CHORUS *(as a bustle ensues)*.
　Shortly shall our noble town
　Be populous and gay,
　High in honor and renown.

PITHETAERUS *(impatiently)*. If I get those wings, it may.

*(EUELPIDES rushes in with a basketful of wings which
PITHETAERUS snatches and doles out to MEN as they pass
by him single file. The MEN affix their new wings as they file
across stage to a promontory and leap off, one by one, rapidly.
EUELPIDES helps PITHETAERUS as BIRDS bring several
more baskets.)*

CHORUS *(during this business)*.
　Now rush them forth, in yellow, red, and blue
　Feathers of every form and size and hue.

PITHETAERUS. Give me a hand, can't you? *(EUELPIDES of-
fers his hand matter-of-factly and gets slapped for it.)*

CHORUS. Where in all this earthly range
　He that wishes for a change
　Can he find a seat,
　Joyous and secure as this,
　Filled with happiness and bliss,
　Such a fair retreat?

PITHETAERUS *(busy distributing wings, to EUELPIDES)*. Ask
that chorus if it has to be so loud, will you? *(EUELPIDES
goes to CHORUS OF BIRDS to shush them but before he can
say anything they double their volume in a great blast which
shakes PITHETAERUS and nearly blows EUELPIDES down.)*

CHORUS. Here is Wisdom and Wit and each exquisite Grace
　And here the unruffled, benevolent face
　Of Quiet, and loving desire.

PITHETAERUS *(shouting)*. It is my desire that you *keep* quiet
so I won't be so ruffled!

CHORUS *(wounded)*. Don't you *like* choruses?

PITHETAERUS *(to EUELPIDES, at the baskets)*. Back to business here.

(As they turn back to the oncoming line of MEN, the POET bursts from the line.)

POET. Wings! Give me wings!

PITHETAERUS. Ye gods, you're back.

POET. On the lightest of wings I shall soar up on high
And lightly from measure to measure I'll fly.

PITHETAERUS. You want wings, do you?

POET. Let me live and let me sing
Like a bird upon the wing.

PITHETAERUS. Oh, stop that! Talk prose! What do you want wings for?

POET. I wish to make a tour among the clouds, collecting images and metaphors and things of that description.

PITHETAERUS. Oh, you pick all your poems out of the clouds, eh?

POET. Oh, yes. All modern poetry is very cloudy. Our most brilliant poems now are those that flap their wings in empty space and are clothed in mist. What we want is a dense obscurity. Listen. I'll give you a sample.

PITHETAERUS *(picking up a pair of wings to hit him with)*. No, you won't.

POET. Now this one is *all* air. Listen.
"Shadowy visions of
Wing-spreading, air-treading
Taper-necked birds..."
(Changing his tactic, PITHETAERUS begins to tickle POET with wings. POET giggles wildly then turns on PITHETAERUS reprovingly.) You're not listening.
(Dancing now.)
"Bounding along on the path to the seas,
Fain I would float on the streams and the breeze..."
(Behind Poet's back, PITHETAERUS signals to several BIRDS, who get a blanket and begin to steal up behind POET.)
"First do I stray on a southerly way,
Then to the northward my body I bear,"

"Cutting a harborless furrow of air,

The air I'll cleave, I'll cleave the sky..."

(PITHETAERUS pushes him over into blanket and they toss him in the air several times.)

PITHETAERUS *(as they let him down)*. How do you like cleaving the air?

POET. If this is how you treat people--

PITHETAERUS. Off with him! Out! *(BIRDS start dragging him out.)*

POET. But where are my wings? Wings! I want wings! *(BIRDS get POET off, and the remaining MEN have now jumped off.)*

PITHETAERUS. Now! Prepare for the feast! Bring me food to roast, and a spit, and the makings of a fire. Oh, dear, I have to do everything.

(As EUELPIDES and BIRDS have scattered in all directions to get supplies, leaving the stage clear, PROMETHEUS, a sneaky, shadowy figure, his cloak about his face and carrying an umbrella, has darted on, looked about the stage suspiciously, checking every nook and corner for someone who may be following him. PITHETAERUS has spotted him, watched him with open-mouthed curiosity, but said nothing. Finally PROMETHEUS comes directly down to PITHETAERUS.)

PROMETHEUS. Is there a god following me?

PITHETAERUS. Not that I know of. What are you all muffled up about?

PROMETHEUS. If only Zeus doesn't see me. That Zeus, always looking. Where is Pithetaerus?

PITHETAERUS. I am Pithetaerus.

PROMETHEUS. Oh, are you? Good boy. *(Taps him approvingly, darts upstage to look around again.)*

PITHETAERUS. Who are you?

PROMETHEUS *(coming back to him)*. What time is it?

PITHETAERUS. Time? Oh, about noon. Who are you?

PROMETHEUS. Only noon? Is that all it is?

PITHETAERUS. How should I know? Who are you?

PROMETHEUS *(after more darting away)*. What's Zeus doing? Is he behind the clouds or is he peeping?

PITHETAERUS *(to audience)*. I don't know about you, but I'm getting bored. *(Shouting at PROMETHEUS.)* WHO ARE YOU?

PROMETHEUS *(coming back to him, mysteriously)*. I shall reveal myself.

PITHETAERUS. Well, take your time. Don't rush. *(PROMETHEUS throws the cloak back from his face. PITHETAERUS throws open his arms and greets him loudly and delightedly.)* Prometheus! My old friend, Prometheus!

PROMETHEUS *(in a panic)*. Shh! Not so loud.

PITHETAERUS. Why, what's the matter, Prometheus?

PROMETHEUS. Shh! Don't mention my name. If Zeus hears you, I'm in for it. He mustn't know I'm here.

PITHETAERUS. Very well.

PROMETHEUS. Here. If you don't mind. Hold the umbrella over me. Then he can't see us.

PITHETAERUS. Right. Right. *(They sit down on edge of stage, umbrella over them, speak quietly.)*

PROMETHEUS. Zeus never liked me, you know.

PITHETAERUS. No.

PROMETHEUS. Ever since I stole that fire from him. Gave it to men. My name has been mud. I still get in up there, but he doesn't trust me.

PITHETAERUS. Of course.

PROMETHEUS. Well. Let me tell you. I've got all the news from Olympus.

PITHETAERUS. Ah?

PROMETHEUS. Just listen.

PITHETAERUS. I'm listening.

PROMETHEUS. Zeus is ruined.

PITHETAERUS *(delighted)*. Ah! Since when?

PROMETHEUS. Since you went to work down here. Built your city. They can't get a message through! Not a thing comes up. No smoke. No incense. Absolutely nothing. They're all on a strict diet up there. The whole bunch. You've done it. *(Shakes Pithetaerus' hand.)*

PITHETAERUS. Good

PROMETHEUS. More than that. Mutiny.

PITHETAERUS. Mutiny up there? *(PROMETHEUS nods knowingly.)* Who?

PROMETHEUS. The new gods. Especially those barbarian gods they took in recently. Hell to pay. Zeus can't meet his commitments. They're furious. Open rebellion. All starving to death. Unless Zeus can get the air lanes open - get traffic started again - he'll be out on his ear. Don't say I told you.

PITHETAERUS. Not a word. But what's Zeus going to do?

PROMETHEUS. That's it. That's what I came for. Zeus is sending a committee. Committee of gods. Ought to be here any minute. I ought to get out of here before they come. One of the barbarian gods is with 'em. Checking up. Anyway. They're going to come to you and sue for peace. Here's the thing. Don't you do it. Don't you agree to a thing unless Zeus acknowledges the rule of the birds. *And...* are you listening? *(PITHETAERUS nods eagerly.)* Don't stop there. To protect yourself... ask for one of the goddesses in marriage. That'll make it stick. Protect your line.

PITHETAERUS. Oh.

PROMETHEUS. Any particular goddess you like?

PITHETAERUS. Why, yes. Yes! There was a little thing in here today. Iris, her name was.

PROMETHEUS. Fine. Ask for Iris. *(Getting up.)* Well, I've got to get out of here. Hell to pay. I only came for a minute. Let you know. But you can count on me. I'm a friend. Steady to the human interest. Always was.

PITHETAERUS. I never eat a roast without thinking of you.

PROMETHEUS. I hate these gods, you know.

PITHETAERUS. Yes, I know.

PROMETHEUS. I'm a regular scourge to them, a regular scourge. Well, bye-bye. Give me the umbrella. If anyone asks, you haven't seen me.

PITHETAERUS. Right.

PROMETHEUS *(at the exit).* Courage. *(As he goes, PITHETAERUS begins hopping around excitedly.)*

PITHETAERUS. Oh, my goodness, I've got to hurry!

(EPOPS and other BIRDS scurry in, carrying an open-fire spit with a pig already on it, together with all the necessary utensils - oversize forks, spoons, salt-cellars, etc.)

PITHETAERUS. Here! Good! *(The spit is mounted downstage, a "fire" is built under it, and several BIRDS remain nearby to help PITHETAERUS as he needs things for the cooking.)*

EPOPS. We have done your bidding, brave leader. Here is food and a fire and everything you need for a banquet.

PITHETAERUS. Fine, fine. Now you must all disappear. I have very important visitors coming. The moment is at hand when our fate will be decided.

EPOPS. I can bring you armies of birds for support.

PITHETAERUS. No, no, no. I must handle this alone. They mustn't think we expect them. Give everything away. I won't even pretend to notice them.

(EUELPIDES runs on.)

PITHETAERUS. Here. Help me here. *(Showing EUELPIDES how to turn spit.)* Epops, you stand by in the rocks and when the meeting is over you can spread the word.

EPOPS. As you say, oh leader! *(EPOPS disappears. EUEL-PIDES is savoring the roasting pig with a loud "Mmmm!" but PITHETAERUS slaps him away.)*

PITHETAERUS. Keep your nose out of that. You'll sniff up all the smell. I'm going to win a war with that smell.

EUELPIDES. We got another war? Where's that fork?

(Snatches up a fork to defend himself with, when there is a sudden smoke puff high up on the rocks. PITHETAERUS glances at it, then, with a great show of indifference, resumes his work with the roast. NEPTUNE, HERCULES, and a BARBARIAN GOD come through the smoke, coughing, sneezing, and flailing with their cloaks to drive the smoke puff away.)

NEPTUNE *(who carries his tined fork and is a pompous, exceedingly dignified god)*. This damn smoke. I wish they'd cut that stuff out. *(Pulling himself together.)* On your dignity, gods.

This is Cloud Cuckoo-land, whither we come as ambassadors. *(Noticing BARBARIAN GOD, whose cloak is dragging sadly and whose general appearance is sloppy indeed.)* You! Barbarian God! Look at your cloak. What a mess. Throw it over your shoulder. *(BARBARIAN GOD does, striking NEPTUNE full in the face with it. NEPTUNE seizes him, forcibly straightens his costume. BARBARIAN GOD maintains an unrelievedly stupid, open-mouthed, deadpan expression.)* What's the matter with you? You are the most uncouth god I ever saw.

BARBARIAN GOD *(low, moronic speaking voice)*. Leave me alone. Leave me alone.

NEPTUNE *(looking at him)*. Oh, democracy! Whither are you leading us?

HERCULES *(bright-faced, simple-minded type)*. Come on. Let's be ambassadors.

NEPTUNE. You will please wait, my dear nephew, Hercules, until you have been instructed. Or did you have some plan of your own?

HERCULES *(pointing to PITHETAERUS, below)*. Certainly. There's the fellow. Let me go strangle him to death.

NEPTUNE. My dear nephew, may I remind you that we are ambassadors of peace.

HERCULES. Sure. When I strangle him, we got peace. What do you want?

BARBARIAN GOD. I wanna go back where I came from.

NEPTUNE *(curious)*. How is it he hasn't noticed our smoke? I hate to put up with that for nothing. *(Clears his throat loudly.)*

PITHETAERUS *(feigning not to notice gods above, now giving directions to EUELPIDES and servant BIRDS who assist him, running for equipment, etc.)* Hand me the grater! Get some spice for the sauce. Where's the cheese? *(NEPTUNE clears his throat again.)* And blow up the fire a little bit. More charcoal. *(NEPTUNE now strides downstage, without going too close to PITHETAERUS. EUELPIDES is backing in his direction at the moment and turns toward him just as NEPTUNE happens to lower his tined fork. EUELPIDES whips out his own fork and takes a dueling stance. HERCULES lifts EUELPIDES bodily out of the way, throws him to one side.)*

NEPTUNE. Mortal! We three who greet you are gods.

PITHETAERUS *(not looking up from his work, waving them away)*. Busy just now. Busy just now. Mixing my sauce. *(To servant BIRD.)* Where are the pickles? Bring me some pickles.

HERCULES *(sniffing and moving closer)*. That sauce smells nice.

PITHETAERUS *(offhand, still not looking up)*. Yes. It's my own recipe.

HERCULES. Uh... what you roasting there?

PITHETAERUS. Pig.

EUELPIDES *(passing, thinking he means him, startled)*. Who?

PITHETAERUS. Later we'll have some nice plump fowl. *(To those around him.)* Salt, please! Get me salt!

HERCULES. I thought you liked birds. Didn't think you'd roast 'em.

PITHETAERUS *(salting the roast)*. Oh, there were some birds who wouldn't join the party. Politically unreliable. *(A servant BIRD is passing and PITHETAERUS salts its tail, too, just for the hell of it.)* Thyme, please! Wild thyme!

NEPTUNE *(impatient and offended)*. Are you going to cook the whole meal before you acknowledge us?

PITHETAERUS. What? *(Looking up now, feigning recognition.)* What's that? Neptune! Well, for heaven's sake! Welcome! Didn't see you.

NEPTUNE. Well. Now that I have your ear... we have been sent by the gods to sue for peace.

PITHETAERUS *(wandering back to his roast, absorbed)*. Yes, yes. Mustn't let this get too done. There's no more olive oil. More olive oil, please.

HERCULES. Oh, you gotta have olive oil. Plenty of olive oil.

NEPTUNE *(turning on his heel and stalking away)*. I told Zeus I didn't want this job. *(Turning back and rapping the floor with his staff.)* Sir! Sir!

PITHETAERUS. What? Oh, yes. Excuse me. *(Wiping his hands on his apron, he casually shifts places with HERCULES in such a way that HERCULES will be placed directly over the roasting pig, inhaling the aroma. PITHETAERUS then crosses to NEPTUNE.)* Wouldn't want to spoil a tasty snack like that.

Personally, I'm hungry. *(Watches for effect of this on NEP-TUNE, who swallows hard, then continues.)*

NEPTUNE. What we have come to say is this. We do not wish to fight you. We are eager to be your friends, to be of service. I am sure we can negotiate. Now on our part we are willing to supply you constantly with warm weather. Further, to see that you always have rain water in your pools. On these points I am prepared to bargain.

PITHETAERUS. Well, now, we're just as interested in peace as you are. We have no plans for aggression, and are also ready to bargain. We have just one condition. Zeus must give up. We take the sceptre. Now if you three will simply agree to this, I shall invite you all to dinner.

HERCULES *(nearly fainting with rapture over the aroma from the roast, speaks quickly)*. I agree.

NEPTUNE. You jackass! *(Strides to him quickly and pulls him away from the roast.)* When are you going to stop being a fathead? Just because you're a fool and a glutton, do you want to dethrone your own father?

HERCULES *(wistfully)*. He'd be mad, wouldn't he?

PITHETAERUS. Now, that's not true at all. You're not facing the facts. The gods would be even *more* powerful if they turned things over to the birds.

EUELPIDES *(quietly to PITHETAERUS, in passing)*. I hope you can sell this one.

PITHETAERUS. How are things now? You gods are stuck up there, behind all those clouds. You don't see *half* of what's going on down below. Men are doing all kinds of things when your backs are turned, especially on cloudy days. But if you put us in charge, we'll watch out for you. Birds get around. Let's say some man down on Earth has promised to offer a sacrifice if he gets a certain favor. Well, he gets the favor and then he forgets all about the sacrifice. We'll keep track of him and, if he doesn't pay up, peck his eyes out. Or at least we'll pick up double the amount of the sacrifice out of his farm yard for you! *(During his speech he has maneuvered NEPTUNE directly over the roast, and NEPTUNE is reacting, too.)*

NEPTUNE *(considering)*. Of course, there's something in what you say--

HERCULES. See? I ain't such a fathead.

PITHETAERUS *(going to BARBARIAN GOD, who has been standing just where he entered, looking stupidly into space, doing nothing)*. How do *you* feel about that?

BARBARIAN GOD. Oh, if it ain't one damn thing it's another.

PITHETAERUS *(to NEPTUNE)*. See? He agrees, too!

NEPTUNE *(looking at BARBARIAN GOD dubiously)*. I'm not sure I can accept that as an official vote. *(Anxious to settle now himself, but worried.)* Oh, Barbarian God, what is your considered opinion?

BARBARIAN GOD. When do we eat?

PITHETAERUS. There you are! Now what do you say?

NEPTUNE. Since I am out-voted, two to one--

EUELPIDES *(looking at BARBARIAN GOD)*. Does he get a whole vote?

PITHETAERUS. Shh! Shh!

NEPTUNE. I consent as well. You shall receive the sceptre. *(With a loud "AHHHH!" from HERCULES, all three GODS start immediately for the spit, drooling. Just as they get there, PITHETAERUS speaks.)*

PITHETAERUS. Oh, I almost forgot. *(They turn to him warily.)* There is one other condition. *(GODS exchange glances.)*

NEPTUNE. And that is?

PITHETAERUS. I must have Iris in marriage. Zeus can have all the others. I only want Iris. *(Pause.)*

NEPTUNE *(pointedly)*. Then you *don't* want peace.

PITHETAERUS. Just little Iris.

NEPTUNE *(imposingly)*. The gods do not marry beneath them! Come, we must go! *(Signals other two GODS and they start away.)*

PITHETAERUS. All right, all right. Doesn't matter to me. *(He goes back to the spit, indifferently.)* How's that gravy coming? That's fine, stir it good. *(GODS are slowing down in their exit, looking back yearningly over their shoulders.)* My, it seems to be turning out just right. Did you ever smell anything like that? *(To EUELPIDES and servant BIRDS.)* Mmm, mmm, here, taste. *(The GODS have tried to force themselves to go, but cannot; they look back to the others relishing a sip of the gravy.)*

HERCULES *(throwing down his club)*. I don't want to go to no war about no woman!

NEPTUNE. It *is* annoying. I never cared much for Iris, anyway. But what can we do?

HERCULES. We can give in.

NEPTUNE. I'm sorry. It's impossible.

HERCULES. You go back. I'm giving in. *(Starting back toward spit.)*

NEPTUNE *(grabbing him)*. Listen, you blockhead. Don't you see? It's not simply a matter of Zeus losing everything. You'd lose everything, too. You're his son and heir.

HERCULES. Oh.

PITHETAERUS *(has been listening and intervenes between NEPTUNE and HERCULES)*. No, you don't. No, you don't. Don't let him take you in with *that* story, friend. Come here. I want a word with you. *(Draws him aside.)* As far as Zeus goes, you may be his son, but you're not his heir.

HERCULES. What do you mean?

PITHETAERUS. I hate to be the one to break it to you. You should have been told. It's been all over Olympus for years.

HERCULES. What has?

PITHETAERUS. I'm sorry, but you're illegitimate.

HERCULES. What!

PITHETAERUS. That's the way it is. You won't get a thing.

NEPTUNE. Here, what are you telling my feeble-minded nephew?

HERCULES. He says I'm a... *(Bursts into tears.)*

PITHETAERUS. I was simply mentioning his origins.

HERCULES *(weeping)*. Uncle Neptune, is it true?

NEPTUNE *(turns away, bites his lip, braces himself)*. Well, Hercules. You're a big boy now. It's time you knew. *(HERCULES bawls louder.)*

EUELPIDES *(to BARBARIAN GOD)*. Poor fellow. He didn't know.

BARBARIAN GOD. What's it to him?

NEPTUNE. Now, now, nephew. Zeus will leave you something in his will.

PITHETAERUS. I'll give you something right now. Roast pig!

HERCULES *(through tears)*. I always knew there was something about me.

PITHETAERUS. Be on my side. I will make you a king and will feed you on bird's milk and honey.

HERCULES. Take me! I wasn't wanted! *(EUELPIDES comforts HERCULES.)*

PITHETAERUS. Neptune! I've got his vote!

NEPTUNE. You haven't got mine.

PITHETAERUS. Then it still depends on old stupid here. *(Turns to BARBARIAN GOD.)* What do you say?

BARBARIAN GOD. Old Stupid votes yes.

PITHETAERUS. We've done it!

HERCULES *(to NEPTUNE)*. And you never told me.

NEPTUNE. All right, all right. I give in. Peace is made.

PITHETAERUS. And just to think - we have the wedding feast all ready!

HERCULES *(to NEPTUNE)*. You go get Iris. I'll keep an eye on the roast.

NEPTUNE. No, you're too fat now.

PITHETAERUS. I have it. *(Getting Hercules' arm.)* You hurry up to Olympus and bring them the news. *That'll* make them respect you! *(HERCULES brightens up.)* Bring me the sceptre... and bring me Iris. *(To EUELPIDES, as HERCULES nods and goes.)* Go get the Birds. Spread the glad tidings. *(To NEPTUNE.)* You. You turn the roast. And don't burn it!

NEPTUNE *(offended)*. I am not the god of the kitchen.

PITHETAERUS. You're taking orders from me now. Remember that! *(Resignedly NEPTUNE goes to the spit and tries to turn the roast with his tines, aloofly. EUELPIDES has rushed in again with EPOPS.)* Oh, Bird-King! The treaty's concluded! The universe is ours!

(The full CHORUS OF BIRDS is in by now.)

CHORUS. Oh, all-successful, more than tongue can tell!
    Oh, this thrice-blessed, winged race of birds
    To have a leader who does so excel

In wisdom and in courage and in power
No man has ever matched him!
*(PITHETAERUS has been benevolently patting various of the
kneeling BIRDS, who bow low before him. He goes off. The
CHORUS OF BIRDS changes to a rapid, suspenseful rhythm,
as the lights change to a mood of revelry.)*
There lies a region out of sight
Far within the realm of night
Far from torch and candlelight...
There in feasts of meal and wine,
Men and demigods may join,
There they banquet, there they dine--

*(The dancing and reveling among the BIRDS has begun.
PROCNE appears and she and EPOPS dance. EUELPIDES
from time to time pursues PROCNE, but is always intercepted
by EPOPS.)*

CHORUS. Whilst the light of day prevails
    Honoring the man - the only man - who never fails!
    *(The revelry reaches a climax, the music stops at a high point,
    and the BIRDS make a royal path.)*
    Stand aside and clear the ground,
    Spreading in a circle round
    With a worthy welcoming
    To salute our noble King!

    (HERALD enters above.)

HERALD. Pithetaerus - the King! *(Coming off his perch, to the
    others.)* And I remembered every word of it.

    *(PITHETAERUS enters, now clad in dazzling robes which look
    quite pretentious on him.)*

CHORUS. Mark his entrance,
    Dazzling all eyes, resplendent as a Star.
    Outshining all the golden lights, that beam

From heaven, even as a summer sun
Blazing at noon!

(IRIS enters, dressed to kill.)

CHORUS. Now to join him by his side
  Comes his happy, lovely bride.
  Oh, the fair delightful face!
  What a figure! What a grace!
  What a presence! What a carriage!
  (IRIS trips over her own train.)
  What a noble worthy marriage.
  (BIRDS have formed a crossed-sword effect as of a military marriage and PITHETAERUS assists IRIS down the path. Leaving it, they go into a little dance of their own.)
  Let the Birds rejoice and sing
  At the wedding of their king,
  Happy to congratulate
  Such a blessing to the state.

(Thunder and lighting. Above, HERCULES enters to present PITHETAERUS with the thunderbolt of Zeus. NEPTUNE and the BARBARIAN GOD join him for the ceremony. The thunderbolt is presented to PITHETAERUS.)

PITHETAERUS. I accept this token of heavenly love.
  (To the CHORUS OF BIRDS.)
  Your music and verse I applaud and admire
  But rouse your invention and, raising it higher,
  Describe me this terrible engine of Zeus...
  ...Now mine--
  The thunder of Earth and the thunder above.
CHORUS. Let us sing of the trophies he brings us from heaven,
  The Earth-crashing thunders, deadly and dire,
  And the lightning's angry flashes of fire--
  (PITHETAERUS is wielding the thunderbolt majestically and lightning and thunder ensues, frightening him.)
  Blaze of the lightning, so terribly beautiful,
  Golden and grand!

Fire-flashing javelin, glittering now in

Our leader's right hand!

(PITHETAERUS quickly gets it into his right hand, a little late.)

Earth-crashing thunder, the hoarsely resounding,

The bringer of showers!

(PITHETAERUS gives the thunderbolt another good shake, just to reassert himself; it brings on such a blast that he quickly and gingerly tosses the thunderbolt away; it is caught accidentally by EUELPIDES who dances uncomfortably about with it and tosses it away himself; it is now caught by the HERALD, who matter-of-factly takes it, as though it were nothing but a prop, and drags it off after him.)

He is our Master, he that is shaking the

Earth with his almighty powers!

PITHETAERUS. Now follow on, dear feathered tribes,

To see us wed, to see us wed

Mount up to Zeus' golden floor

But watch your head, yes, watch your head!

(BIRDS are forming an exit processional as PITHETAERUS turns to IRIS.)

And oh, my darling, reach thine hand

And take my wing and dance with me,

And I will lightly bear thee up

And carry thee, and carry thee.

(He picks her up - it requires a mighty effort - and begins to ascend the rocks with her. See Production Notes. **)

CHORUS. Raise the joyous paean-cry,

Raise the song of victory.

Io Paean, alalalae

Mightiest of powers, to thee!

(The BIRDS dance off, higher and higher, on the rocks as the lights fade, until only Procne's silhouette is visible, and she, too, disappears.)

CURTAIN

PRODUCTION NOTES

*(Page 39) Though this business was not used in the original production, the real estate man may have a fleet of assistants who immediately begin to tape and mark out the space on stage, planting signs reading *"Lot One," "Lot Two," "Dead End"* - at a high peak - and so on.

**(Page 70) In the original production, these two were blocked out for a moment during the processional and a dummy, identically dressed, was substituted for Iris, so that on the last line, Pithetaerus could mightily seem to hoist Iris by one hand over his head and carry her off. Where this business is impractical, it is possible to extend the earlier business of his trying to pick her up, whereupon an escort of Birds takes over for him, raising her up and bearing her off as though on a litter, with PITHETAERUS following in state.

THE SETTING: Limitless sky in the background. The rock formations should afford six or seven varied entrances, at different heights, with stair-like formations to connect the acting levels. At one side a little bridge between two pinnacles. A high point of the stage at DR is so arranged as to be useful to Pithetaerus as a sort of pulpit.

Various gnarled and barren trees, especially on the upper reaches of the stage, including one tree which is practical for a perch and may occasionally be used by one of the Birds.

At DL, there is a gap in the rock formation which seems to lead downward and which is used for any ascent from the earth.

In a crevice somewhere upstage is concealed Procne's nest, if possible behind a movable scrim which is identical with the other rock surfaces when not lighted from within.

The small birds carried by Pithetaerus and Euelpides are so constructed as to fit over one arm, like a sleeve. Their heads can then be manipulated by the actors' fingers.

CHARACTER NOTES: (POET) is dressed in rags, with long, flowing hair. (IRIS) has a Brooklyn accent.